Robert Southwell

The Complete Works of R. Southwell

With Life and Death

Robert Southwell

The Complete Works of R. Southwell
With Life and Death

ISBN/EAN: 9783337004569

Printed in Europe, USA, Canada, Australia, Japan

Cover: Foto ©ninafisch / pixelio.de

More available books at **www.hansebooks.com**

THE COMPLETE WORKS

OF

R. SOUTHWELL, S.J.,

WITH LIFE AND DEATH.

NEW EDITION.

LONDON:
D. STEWART, WARWICK CHAMBERS,
PATERNOSTER ROW, E.C.
1876.

CONTENTS.

	Page
PREFACE	v
Memorial Introduction; The Life	vii
SAINT PETER'S COMPLAINT	7
Mary Magdalen's Blush	43
Mary Magdalen's Complaint at Christ's Death	45
Times go by Turns	47
Look Home	49
Fortune's Falsehood	51
Scorn not the Least	53
A Child my Choice	55
Content and Rich	57
Loss in Delay	60
Love's Servile Lot	62
Life is but Loss	66
I die alive	68
What Joy to Live	69
Life's Death, Love's Life	71
At Home in Heaven	73
Lewd Love is Loss	75
Love's Garden Grief	77
From Fortune's Reach	79
A Fancy turned to a Sinner's Complaint	81
David's Peccavi	88
Sin's Heavy Load	90
Joseph's Amazement	92
New Prince, New Pomp	96
The Burning Babe	98
New Heaven, new War	100
MÆONIÆ	103
Conception of Our Lady	105

CONTENTS.

	Page
Our Lady's Nativity	106
Our Lady's Espousals	107
Our Lady's Salutation	108
The Visitation	109
The Nativity of Christ	110
The Circumcision	112
The Epiphany	113
The Presentation	115
The Flight into Egypt	116
Christ's return out of Egypt	117
Christ's Childhood	118
Christ's Bloody Sweat	119
Christ's Sleeping Friends	121
The Virgin Mary to Christ on the Cross	123
Saint Thomas of Aquines Hyme Read on Corpus Christy Daye	125
Saint Peter's Afflicted Mind	129
Saint Peter's Remorse	131
Man to the Wound in Christ's Side	134
Upon the Image of Death	136
A Vale of Tears	139
The Prodigal Child's Soul Wrack	143
Man's Civil War	146
Seek Flowers of Heaven	148

ADDITIONAL POEMS.

Decease, Release. Dum Morior, Orior	153
I die without Desert	155
Of the Blessed Sacrament of the Altar	157
The Death of Our Lady	161
The Assumption of Our Lady	162
Verses appended to the "Triumphs over Death"	163

VERSES PREFIXED TO "SHORT RULES OF GOOD LIFE."

1. To the Christian Reader	165
2. A Preparative to Prayer	166
3. The Effects of Prayer	167
4. Ensamples of our Saviour	168

APPENDIX.

PREFACE.

IN presenting to the public the first cheap edition of the Poems of the meek and holy martyr, Robert Southwell, very few words of preface are necessary.

The work has long been known and appreciated by Scholars and Critics.

The Poems of Father Southwell are however eminently adapted for general use.

His touching aphorisms, his sweet quaint images, should make them familiar in every christian household.

The Bard of Bards, Shakspeare himself, never gave a more wholesome lesson, than is couched in these simple lines :—

"A chance may win, that by mischance was lost;
The well that holds no great, takes little fish;
In some things all, in all things none are crossed,
Few all they need, but none have all they wish;
Unmeddled joys here to no man befall,
Who least hath some, who most hath never all."

Let the children lisp the Poetry of Southwell, and lay it to their hearts. It has uses for this world, as well as for the next.

MEMOIR OF THE REV. ROBERT SOUTHWELL, S.J.

ROBERT SOUTHWELL, the third son of Richard Southwell, Esq., of Horsham St. Faith's,* in the county of Norfolk, a gentleman of ancient family, and ancestor of the present Viscount Southwell, was born there about the year 1562.† While an infant yet in the cradle, he was stolen by a gipsy or vagrant, who substituted for him her own child: but the theft was speedily discovered, and the woman, apprehended at a short distance from his parental mansion, confessed to have been prompted to the crime for the sake of

---

* The site of the Benedictine priory of Horsham St. Faith's, about five miles from Norwich, with the lordship, lands, &c., were granted *circa* 36 Hen. VIII. to Sir Richard Southwell of Wood Rising in com. Norfolk, and Edw. Ebrington. In 1588 it was held by Richard Southwell (father of the poet), and by him sold to Sir Henry Hobart, afterwards Chief Justice of the Common Pleas.—*Blomefield's History of Norfolk, by Parkin*, x. 441.

† Pits (who is followed by Fuller) erroneously says that he was born in Suffolk: but he adds:—"Romæ mihi familiariter notus erat. In philosophia atque etiam in theologia non pœnitendos fecerat progressus. Elegantiam maternæ linguæ tum prosa, tum versu satis avidè sectabatur. Et in patriam

gain. This circumstance Southwell gratefully remembered in after years. "What," says he, "if I had remained with the vagrant? how abject! how destitute of the knowledge or reverence of God! in what debasement of vice, in what great peril of crimes, in what indubitable risk of a miserable death and eternal punishment I should have been!" And his first care upon entering upon his mission was to convert to the Church the female who had been the instrument of detecting the theft.* At the age of fifteen he was sent to Paris for education, and his religious instruction was superintended by Father Thomas Darbyshire, (nephew to the celebrated Bishop Bonner), one of the earliest Englishmen who became members of the Society of Jesus. From his example, he probably derived the ardent zeal and desire to enter that distinguished order, which is manifested in his beautiful complaint of the delay in his admission,—"divulsum ab illo corpore, in quo posita sunt mea vita, meus amor, totum cor meum, omnesque effectus,"—and which may be seen in the History of the English Mission by Father Henry More.†

---

missus illud talentum suum et in concionibus et in libris scriptis exercuisse non illaudabiliter dicitur."—*De Illust. Angliæ Scriptor*, ed. 1619, p. 794.

* Mori, Hist. Prov. Angl. Soc. Jesu, p. 172.

† Ibid. p. 173. Tanner (Soc. Jesu Martyr, p. 30) thus speaks of his love for the Order:—"Nescio an quis alius unquam post sanctissimum Parentem ejus Ignatium, majorem de Societate Jesu sensum, majorem vocationis suæ foverit æstimationem, quàm Robertus Southwellus ..... Scripsit

REV. ROBERT SOUTHWELL.

It is stated by Bishop Chaloner, in his Memoirs of Missionary Priests, that Southwell was for some time an *alumnus* of the English College at Douay. He could not however have long studied there, since he went to Rome, and was received into the Society on the Vigil of St. Luke (17th October), 1578, ere he had completed his seventeenth year.

After his reception, he spent a considerable portion of his noviciate at Tournay, in Belgium, lest, being unused to the extreme warmth of Italy, his ardent zeal, united to the influence of the atmosphere, might have affected or destroyed his constitution.* From Tournay, returning to Rome, he entered upon the course of philosophy and theology; in which he acquitted himself so brilliantly, that, after completing his studies, he was appointed Prefect of the English College there.†

---

aliquando in sua ad socios Romam epistola S. Xaverius, æternum animæ suæ exitium imprecans, si unquam ab amore dilectissimæ suæ religionis desciscerei : *si oblitus,* inquit, *fuero tui, O Societas Jesu, oblivioni detur dextera mea.* Sed an non sublimes ejus de hoc ordine conceptus adæquârit, si non superâret Robertus, clarissimo in Anglia gentis Southwelliæ natus sanguine, ex his sua propriâ manu consignavit, patebit."

* "Ne videlicet ardentem sanctis desideriis juvenem, immoderatis Italiæ æstibus nondum parem, duo in uno corpore calores opprimerent, utque tam præclaris dotibus ornato, et qui per ardorem quærendi spem excitaverat eximia quædam adipiscendi, non sola Roma nobilitaretur."—*Ibid.* p. 177.

† "Romam Tornaco rursus vocatus ad philosophos, theologosque audiendos, neque ingenio, neque industria, neque laude studiorum, aut fructu, neque vita cum virtute acta cuiquam se passus est esse inferiorem. Et ingenii quidem et industriæ laus in universæ philosophiæ decretis propugnandis

Having been ordained priest in 1584, his earnest desire to devote himself to the cure of souls in England was exemplified in a letter to the General, of 20th Feb. in the following year, wherein his future martyrdom seems rather to have been anticipated, than merely referred to as a simple possibility. The same dauntless devotion to duty is expressed in another letter to his late spiritual director, from Porto, 5th July, 1586, while on his way to discharge these earnestly-sought functions, to which in that year he had been appointed with Father Henry Garnet (himself the well known subsequent martyr), and in company with whom he had left Rome, on the 8th of May previously. These may be seen in Father More's History, so frequently referred to.* Southwell and his companion reached England on the 7th July following.

The advent of these distinguished men was during a most disturbed period, when the course of political intrigues, for and against the unfortunate Queen of Scots, had established a reign of terror over the Catholic community.† Already' had

---

enituit; tum etiam, cùm post decursum theologiæ stadium, aliorum studiis est præfectus in Anglicano de urbe Seminario; in quo juventus id temporis copiosissima, et ingeniorum varietate, et splendore florentissima non facilè nisi ab omnibus doctrinæ præsidiis ornato atque instructo ducebatur."—*Ibid.* p. 179.

* Pp. 182, 183

† As Father More truly says:—" Ea enim erant tempora in quibus malitia vires omnes suas intendebat ad perniciem, et quidquid vel potentia vel arte poterat, id omne et subdole machinabatur, et furore percita exequebatur."

seventy priests been banished; Francis Throckmorton and Dr. Parry had fallen on the scaffold, the confederacy of Babington and his friends was rapidly leading them to a similar fate, and Philip, Earl of Arundel, was a prisoner in the Tower. Great, therefore, was the danger which these holy men incurred by landing; yet they fortunately at that time escaped, and were hospitably received and entertained for some months in the house of William, 3rd Lord Vaux of Harrowden,* when the confessor of the Countess of Arundel (wife of Philip aforesaid) chancing to die, Father Southwell was appointed domestic chaplain and confessor to her ladyship in his place. It was while in her family that he composed for the Earl's use the "Consolation for Catholics," and the two following letters, painfully illustrative of the period and written shortly before his own sufferings, which are translated from the History of the Persecutions in England, by Didacus Yepes, Bishop of Tarrazona, lib. v. cap. 6, p. 647.

I.

"As yet we are alive and well, being unworthy, it seems, of prisons. We have oftener sent than received letters from your parts, though they are not sent without difficulty; and some, we know, have been lost.

---

* At Hackney.

"The condition of Catholic recusants here is the same as usual, deplorable and full of fears and dangers, more especially since our adversaries have looked for wars. As many of ours as are in chains rejoice, and are comforted in their prisons; and they that are at liberty set not their hearts upon it, nor expect it to be of long continuance. All, by the great goodness and mercy of God, arm themselves to suffer any thing that can come, how hard soever it may be, as it shall please our Lord; for whose greater glory and the salvation of their souls, they are more concerned than for any temporal losses.

"A little while ago they apprehended two priests, who have suffered such cruel usages in the prison of Bridewell as can scarce be believed. What was given them to eat was so little in quantity, and withal, so filthy and nauseous, that the very sight of it was enough to turn their stomachs. The labours to which they obliged them were continual and immoderate, and no less in sickness than in health; for with hard blows and stripes they forced them to accomplish their task, how weak soever they were. Their beds were dirty straw, and their prison most filthy.

"Some are there hung up, for whole days, by the hands, in such a manner that they can but just touch the ground with the tops of their toes. In fine, they that are kept in that prison truly live *in lacu miseriæ et in luto fæcis*, Psalm xxxix. This purgatory we are looking for every hour, in which

Topcliffe and Young, the two executioners of the Catholics, exercise all kinds of torments. But come what pleaseth God, we hope we shall be able to bear all *in Him that strengthens us.* In the mean time we prey, that *they may be put to confusion who work unjustly*: and that *the Lord may speak peace to His people,* Psalms xxiv. and lxxxiv, that, as the royal prophet says, *His glory may dwell in our land.* I most humbly recommend myself to the holy sacrifices of your Reverence and of all our friends. *January* 16, 1590."

II.

" We have written many letters, but, it seems, few have come to your hands. We sail in the midst of these stormy waves with no small danger; from which, nevertheless, it has pleased our Lord hitherto to deliver us.

" We have altogether, with much comfort, renewed the Vows of the Society, according to our custom, spending some days in exhortations and spiritual conferences. *Aperuimus ora, et attraximus Spiritum.* It seems to me that I see the beginning of a religious life set on foot in England, of which we now sow the seeds with tears, that others hereafter may with joy carry in the sheaves to the heavenly granaries.

" We have sung the Canticles of the Lord in a strange land, and in this desert we have sucked honey from the rock, and oil from the hard stone. But these our joys ended in sorrow, and sudden fears dispersed us into different places: but, in fine, we were more afraid than hurt, for we all escaped. I, with another of ours, seeking to avoid Scylla, had like to have fallen into Charybdis; but, by the mercy of God, we passed betwixt them both without being shipwrecked, and are now sailing in a safe harbour.

"In another of mine I gave an account of the late martyrdoms of Mr. Bayles and Mr. Horner,* and of the edification which the people received from their holy ends. With such dews as these the Church is watered, *ut in stillicidiis hujusmodi lætetur germinans*, Psal. lxiv. We also look for the time (if we are not unworthy of so great a glory) when our day (like that of the hired servant) shall come. In the meanwhile I recommend myself very much to your Reverence's prayers, that the Father of Lights may enlighten us, and confirm us with His principal Spirit. Given March 8, 1590."

One of his earliest cares, upon entering on his mission, was to bring back his own father to his religious duties. Mr. Southwell, a gentleman of opulence, had married a lady of the Court, formerly—according to More—the instructress of Queen Elizabeth in the Latin language; and this connection, as well as his wealth (which seldom pays the turnpike to heaven), appears to have made him a time-server, and, although a believer in the

---

* See Bp. Chaloner's *Memoirs of Missionary Priests*, i. 249, ed. 1741.

REV. ROBERT SOUTHWELL.

doctrines of the Church, an absentee from its observations. From this state of enslavement to expediency and mammon, Father Southwell naturally sought to emancipate his parent; and his desire was happily fulfilled, through the instrumentality *(inter alia)* of a letter printed at the end of this Volume. That which follows it, addressed to his brother, shews that he also had required and received the spiritual attentions of the future martyr.

Although fully engaged with his sacerdotal duties, yet, by his accurate and strict distribution of time, Father Southwell was enabled to make his abilities conducive both to the intellectual recreation and to the spirtual edification of his countrymen; as the contents of the present volume and his other works amply shew. These were all composed during his residence with Lady Arundel.

He had in this manner, for six years, pursued, with very great success, the objects of his mission, when these were abruptly terminated by his foul betrayal into the hands of his enemies in 1592. The circumstances were as follow:—

There was resident at Uxendon,* near Harrow

---

* "The manor of Woxindon, now called Uxendon, in this parish, was formerly the property of the Travers family, from whom it passed to Sir Nicholas Brembre, about the year 1376. Some years afterwards, in consequence of a judgment against this Sir Nicholas in parliament, it became forfeited to the crown, and was granted by King Richard, *anno* 1394, in consideration of the sum of £40 to Thomas Godelac and Joan his wife. It seems probable that it passed from the family of

on the Hill, in Middlesex, a Catholic family of the name of Bellamy, whom Southwell was in the habit of visiting and providing with religious instruction when he exchanged his ordinary close confinement for a purer atmosphere. One of the daughters, Ann, had in her early youth exhibited marks of the most vivid and unshakeable piety; but, having been committed to the Gatehouse of Westminster, her faith gradually departed, and along with it her virtue. For, having formed an intrigue with the Keeper of the prison, she subsequently married him, and by this step forfeited all claim which she had by law or favour upon her father. In order, therefore, to obtain some fortune, she resolved to take advantage of the Act of 27 Elizabeth, which made the harbouring of a priest treason, with confiscation of the offender's goods. Accordingly she sent a messenger to Southwell,

---

Godelac to that of Bellamy" (see Appendix V.), "in consequence of an intermarriage; for it appears that the Bellamys of Uxendon, who were for many years proprietors of this and other large estates in Harrow, quartered the arms of Godelac.

"It is related in the chronicles, that Babington, who, with other conspirators, had laid a plot against Queen Elizabeth and the state, in the year 1586, when he found that the conspiracy was detected, being a very handsome man, disfigured his face with the juice of green walnuts, and wandered about in that disguise with his associates till they were half starved, in which condition they were received at Bellamy's house near Harrow, where they were at length discovered, and being brought to London, were executed with circumstances of unusual severity. Jerome Bellamy suffered death also for concealing them; his brother destroyed himself in prison. The manor of Uxendon was aliened by the Bellamys to the Page

urging him to meet her on a certain day and hour at her father's house, whither he, either in ignorance of what had happened, or under the impression that she sought his spiritual assistance through motives of penitence, went at the appointed time. In the meanwhile, having apprised her husband of this, as also of the place of concealment in her father's house and the mode of access, he conveyed the information to Topcliffe,* an implacable persecutor and denouncer of the Catholics, who, with a band of his satellites, surrounded the premises, broke open the house, arrested his Reverence, and carried him off in open day exposed to the gaze of the populace. He was taken in the first instance to Topcliffe's house, where during a few weeks he was put to the torture ten times with such dreadful severity, that Southwell, complaining of it to his judges, declared in the name of God that death would have been more preferable. The manner in which he was agonized may be seen in Tanner's

---

family in the early part of the last century, and is now (1795) the property of Richard Page, Esq., of Wimbley." (Lysons' Environs, ii. 565.) At present (1856) it belongs to Henry Young, Esq., of Sudbury: no vestige of the mansion exists.

* See notice of this bloodhound in Lodge's *Illustrations of British History*, ii. p. 125, octavo edition. The miscreant had permission from the Queen's Council to torture in any manner, and to any extent short of death, the unfortunate victims of his generally too successful search. He was frequently heard to say that nothing gave him greater delight than the torturing and butchering of Catholics; and that, if his power was equal to his will, his dearest pleasure would be to blow every Jesuit to powder in the air.

"Societas Jesu Martyr." But all was to no purpose; the sufferer maintained an inflexible silence; nothing could shake his constancy, and the tormentors affirmed that he resembled a post rather than a man.* He was then transferred to the same Gatehouse which was kept by the husband of the wretch who had betrayed him;† and after being confined there for two months, was removed to the Tower, and thrown into a dungeon so filthy and noisome, that, when brought forth at the end of a month to be examined, his clothes were covered with vermin. Whereupon his father presented a petition to Elizabeth, humbly entreating that if his son had committed anything for which by the laws he had deserved it, he might suffer death; if not, as he was a gentleman, he hoped her Majesty would be pleased to order that he should be treated as such, and not be confined in that

---

* As to his fortitude we have the admiring testimony of Cecil :—" Let antiquity boast of its Roman heroes, and the patience of captives in torments : our own age is not inferior to it, nor do the minds of the English cede to the Romans. There is at present confined one Southwell, a Jesuit, who, thirteen times most cruelly tortured, cannot be induced to confess anything, not even the colour of the horse, whereon on a certain day he rode, lest from such indication his adversaries might conjecture in what house, or in company of what Catholics, he that day was."—MORE, *ut supra*, p. 193.

† What portion this vile woman received of her father's escheated property does not appear; but Father More states that he had seen the poor old man in Belgium, exiled and beggared, and dragging out a precarious existence on some miserable pittance. This seems somewhat at variance with what is said by Lysons in a previous note, p. xxiii.

filthy hole.* The Queen, in consequence, ordered that he should be better lodged, and gave his father permission to supply him with clothing, necessaries, and books; of which latter, the only ones which he asked for were the Bible and the works of St. Bernard. During all his protracted confinement, although his sister Mary, who was married to a gentleman of the name of Bannister, had occasional access to him, he never discoursed on anything but religion.†

After three years' close detention in the Tower, Father Southwell wrote to the Lord Treasurer, Cecil, humbly entreating that he might either be brought to trial, to answer for himself, or, at least, that his friends might have permission to come to see him. Whereupon, it is said, that Cecil replied to the effect that "if he was in so much haste to be hanged, he should have his desire." Be this as it may, on the 18th of February, 1594-5, he was taken from the Tower to Newgate, and

---

* Chaloner's *Memoirs of Missionary Priests*, i. 325, ed. 1741.

† From a letter of one John Danyell, addressed to Sir Robert Cecil, 5 Aug. 1595 (State Paper Office, Domestic, No. 200), it would seem that he was one of the diabolical emissaries of the time. He says:—" At the arrayment of Yorke, Williams and Southwell the Jesuite, John Danyell was nomynated to have been the first discoverer of these late practizes intended against her hyghness and her dominions, myself standing by. I refere me to the reports of my veray good lo. yor. father, the lievetenant of the Tower, Mr. Toplyffe and Mr. Justice Young yf he were alyve, how reddy I was sins my coming to delyver my knowledge of all such as came or weare to come for any ill entent, and will so contynue while I lyve with'respect

thrown into a subterraneous dungeon there, (called *Limbo* from its darkness and offensiveness,) where he was detained three days and then removed to Westminster for trial. On the 21st he was placed at the bar, before Chief Justice Popham, Justice Owen, Baron Evans, and Sergeant Daniel; Sir Edward Coke, Solicitor General, appearing for the prosecution. To the usual question Father Southwell, of course, pleaded not guilty to the charge of treason, but fully and distinctly admitted (his only crime) that he was a priest, and had returned to his own country simply to administer the Sacraments to those of his religion who might desire them, and perform the ordinary duties of a clergyman of the Church of Rome. The Chief Justice and Coke having, in their accustomed style, addressed the Jury, a verdict of guilty, necessarily in accordance with the existing statute, was returned. A succinct report of the proceedings may be seen in the Memoirs of Bishop Chaloner previously referred to: the prisoner's noble defence in the history of Father More.

---

to persons. In case that old George Herbert who was with Charles Arrondell beyond the seas be (as I hear say) apprehended and comytted to the Tower, he can discover as moche as Holt the Jesuite, S. Willm. Taylor and Hughe Owen; yf he hathe or will not of himselfe like a good subject delivir his knowledge plainlie and truelie, and that her Matie and y^r. honors be not sufficientlie instructed to examyne him uppon certaine points I will deliver y^r. honor in writing by way of Interrogatory so moche as I know, and will confront him or any other for her Maties' service. I was never a traytor in any country nor beyond the seas," &c. &c. &c.

At daybreak of the 22nd the chief jailor apprised him that he was to die that morning. Southwell embraced him, and said, "You could not bring me more joyful tidings. I regret that I have nothing left of greater value, but accept this nightcap as evidence of my gratitude." This gift the jailor held in such estimation that, while he lived, nothing could induce him to part with it. Being placed upon a hurdle, he was drawn to the place of Execution at Tyburn. On arriving there, when unbound, he wiped from his face the mud which the jolting of the sledge had cast upon it, with a neckerchief, which he threw to one of the Society whom he recognized in the crowd, by whom it was given to Father Garnet, from whose hands it passed to Acquaviva, at that time General of the Order. He then, after making the sign of the Cross, addressed the multitude, who, by their silence and decorum, testified their admiration of the martyr, in the following words, beginning with those of the Apostle :—

"'Whether we live, we live unto the Lord ; or whether we die we die unto the Lord. Therefore, whether we live or whether we die, we are the Lord's.' Of which most clement God and Father of Mercies, through the blood of Jesus Christ, I in the first place crave forgiveness for all things wherein I may have offended since my infancy. Then as regards the Queen (to whom I have never done nor wished any evil), I have daily prayed for her, and now with all my heart do pray, that from His great mercy, through the wounds and most worthy merits of Christ His son, He may grant that she may use the ample gifts and endowments wherewith He has endowed her, to the immortal glory of His name, the prosperity of the whole nation, and the eternal welfare of her soul and body. For my most miserable and with all tears to be pitied country, I pray the light of truth, whereby the darkness of ignorance being dispelled, it may learn in and above all things to praise God, and seek its eternal good in the right way. And since I perceive that I am not permitted to speak at greater length, I deliver my soul into the hands of God my Creator, earnestly beseeching Him that He may preserve and strengthen it with His grace, and grant it to continue faithful in this final conflict. For what may be done to my body I have no care. But since death, in the admitted cause for which I die, cannot be otherwise than most happy and desirable, I pray the God of all comfort that it may be to me the complete cleansing of my sins and a real solace and increase of faith and constancy to others. For I die because I am a Catholic priest, elected into the Society of Jesus in my youth; nor has any other thing, during the last three years in which I have been imprisoned, been charged against me. This death, therefore, although it may now seem base and ignominious, can to no rightly-thinking person appear doubtful but that it is beyond measure an eternal weight of glory to be wrought in us, who look not to the things which are visible, but to those which are unseen."

This speech, firmly delivered, moved the audience to much commiseration, notwithstanding the interruptions of some of the teachers of Protestant opinions among them, whom Southwell rebuked. "Whatever," said he, pointing to them, "these men may say or do, I live and die a Catholic: this, you who are Catholics here, I take to witness." Then recollecting himself, he prepared for his approaching end, frequently ejaculating, "Holy Mary, Mother of God, and all saints pray for me;" and, signing himself with the cross, "Into thy hands, O Lord, I commend my spirit; thou hast redeemed me, O Lord God of truth, my God and all; God be merciful to me a sinner," &c. At length, the horses being started and the car removed from under his feet, he continued to beat his breast and make the sign of the cross, until the executioner, who had so awkwardly applied the noose as to prevent his speedy strangulation, pulled him by the legs to ease his agony. The matyr's behaviour had such an effect on the spectators, that when, in terms of his sentence, the executioner wished to cut him down alive, neither they nor the magistrate who superintended the judicial murder would permit him to do so. When he was dead, his countenance exhibited no change, neither did the halter leave its ordinary marks of discoloration; and when his body was partitioned, the heart leaped from the dissector's hand, and, by its throbbing, seemed to repel the flames, as if expressing with the Psalmist, "My heart and my flesh shall exult in the living God." Lord Mountjoy,* who happened to be present, was so struck by the martyr's constancy, that he exclaimed, "May my soul be with this man's!" and he assisted in restraining those who would have cut the rope while he was still in life.

So perished Father Southwell, at thirty-three years of age, and so unhappily have perished many of the wise and virtuous of the earth, conscious of suffering in the best of causes. He seemed to have met death without terror; to have received the Crown of Martyrdom, not only with resignation, but with joy.

Indeed, persecution and martyrdom, torture! and death! must have been frequent subjects of his contemplation. His brethren of the priesthood were falling around him, and he himself assumed the character of a comforter and encourager to those who remained. Life's uncertainty and the world's vanity, the crimes and follies of humanity, and the consolations and glories of religion, are the constant themes of his writings, both in prose and verse; and the kindliness and benignity of his nature, and the moral excellence of his character are diffused alike over both.

---

* Charles Blount, 8th Baron Mountjoy.

THE AUTHOR TO HIS LOVING COUSIN.

POETS, by abusing their talents, and making the follies and feignings of love the customary subject of their base endeavours, have so discredited this faculty, that a poet, a lover, and a liar, are by many reckoned but three words of one signification. But the vanity of men cannot counterpoise the authority of God, who delivered many parts of Scripture in verse, and, by his apostle willing us to exercise our devotion in hymns and spiritual songs, warranteth the art to be good and the use allowable. And therefore not only among the heathens, whose Gods were chiefly canonized by their poets, and their paynim divinity oracled in verse; but even in the Old and New Testament it hath been used by men of the greatest piety in matters of most devotion. Christ himself, by making an hymn the conclusion of his last supper, and the prologue to the first pageant of his passion, gave his Spouse a method to imitate, as in the office of the Church it appeareth; and to all men a pattern, to know the true use of this measured style.

But the devil, as he affecteth deity and seeketh to have all the compliments of divine honour applied to his service, so hath he among the rest possessed also most Poets with his idle fancies. For in lieu of solemn and devout matters, to which in duty they owe their abilities, they now busy themselves in expressing such passions as serve only for testimonies to what unworthy affections they have wedded their wills. And, because the best course to let them see the error of their works is to weave a new web in their own loom, I have here laid a few coarse threads together to invite some skilfuller wits to go forward in the same, or to begin some finer piece, wherein it may be seen how well verse and virtue suit together.

Blame me not, good Cousin, though I send you a blame-worthy present, in which the most that can be commended is the good will of the writer; neither art nor invention giving it any credit. If in me this be a fault, you cannot be faultless that did importune me to commit it, and therefore you must bear part of the penance when it shall please sharp censures to impose it. In the mean time, with many good wishes, I send you these few ditties; add you the tunes, and let them, I pray you, be still a part in all your music.

TO THE READER.

DEAR eye, that dost peruse my muses still,
   With easy censure deem of my delight;
   Give sob'rest count'nance leave sometime to smile,
And gravest wits to take a breathing flight:
Of mirth to make a trade may be a crime,
But tired sprites for mirth must have a time.

The lofty eagle soars not still above,
High flights will force her from the wing to stoop;
And studious thoughts at times men must remove,
Lest by excess before the time they droop:
In coarser studies 'tis a sweet repose,
With poets pleasing vein to temper prose.

Prophane conceits and feignèd fits I fly;
Such lawless stuff doth lawless speeches fit,
With David, verse to virtue I apply,
Whose measure best with measured words doth fit;
It is the sweetest note that man can sing
When grace in virtue's key tunes nature's string.

RURSUS AD EUNDEM.

DEAR eye, that deignest to let fall a look
 On these sad memories of Peter's plaints,
 Muse not to see some mud in clearest brook;
They once were brittle mould that now are saints.
Their weakness is no warrant to offend;
Learn by their faults what in thine own to mend.

If Justice' even hand the balance held,
Where Peter's sins and ours were made the
 weights,—
Ounce for his drachm, pound for his ounce we
 yield,—
His ship would groan to feel some sinners'
 freights.
So ripe is vice, so green is virtue's bud,
The world doth wax in ill, but wane in good.

This makes my mourning muse dissolve in tears,
This themes my heavy pen,—too plain in prose;
Christ's thorn is sharp, no head his garland
 wears;
Still finest wits are 'stilling Venus' rose:
In paynim toys the sweetest veins are spent;
To Christian works few have their talents lent.

RURSUS AD EUNDEM.

Licence my single pen to seek a phere;
You heavenly sparks of wit shew native light,
Cloud not with misty loves your orient clear,
Sweet flights you shoot, learn once to level right.
Favour my wish, well-wishing works no ill;
I move the suit, the grant rests in your will.

SAINT PETER'S COMPLAINT,

MARY MAGDALEN'S TEARS,

WITH OTHER WORKS OF

THE AUTHOR

R. S.

LONDON:
PRINTED BY J. HAVILAND, AND
SOLD BY ROBERT ALLOTT.
1634.

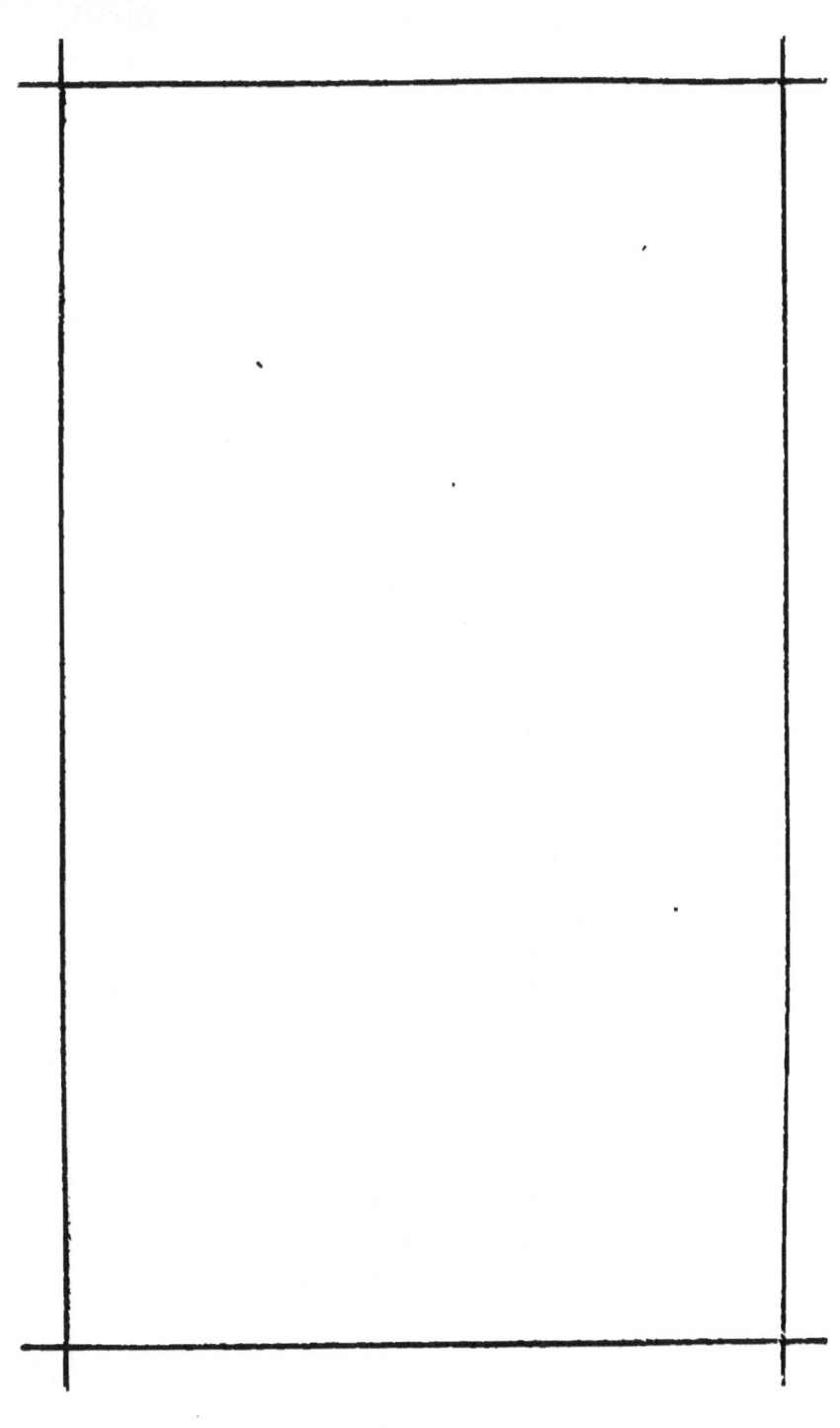

SAINT PETER'S COMPLAINT.

LAUNCH forth, my soul, into a main of tears,
   Full fraught with grief, the traffic of thy mind;
Torn sails will serve thoughts rent with guilty fears,
   Give care the stern, use sighs instead of wind:
Remorse thy pilot, thy misdeed thy card,
Torment thy haven, shipwreck thy best reward.

Shun not the shelf of most deserved shame,
   Stick in the sands of agonizing dread;
Content thee to be storms' and billows' game,
   Divorced from grace, thy soul to penance wed:
Fly not from foreign ills, fly from the heart,
Worse than the worst of ills is that thou art.

Give vent unto the vapours of thy breast,
   That thicken in the brims of cloudy eyes;
Where sin was hatch'd, let tears now wash the nest,
   Where life was lost, recover life with cries;
Thy trespass foul, let not thy tears be few,
Baptize thy spotted soul in weeping dew.

Fly mournful plaints, the echoes of my ruth,
   When screeches in my frightened conscience
      ring,
Sob out my sorrows, fruits of mine untruth,
   Report the smart of sin's infernal sting;
Tell hearts that languish in the sorriest plight,
There is on earth a far more sorry wight.

A sorry wight, the object of disgrace,
   The monument of fear, the map of shame,
The mirror of mishap, the stain of place,
   The scorn of time, the infamy of fame,
An excrement of earth, to heaven hateful,
To man injurious, to God ungrateful.

Ambitious heads, dream you of Fortune's pride,
   Fill volumes with your forgèd goddess' praise;
You Fancy's drudges, plunged in Folly's tide,
   Devote your fabling wits to lovers' lays:
Be you, O sharpest griefs that ever rung!
Text to my thoughts, theme to my plaining tongue.

Sad subject of my sin hath stored my mind,
   With everlasting matter of complaint;
My themes an endless alphabet do find,
   Beyond the pangs which Jeremy doth paint;
That eyes with errors may just measure keep,
Most tears I wish, that have most cause to weep.

ST. PETER'S COMPLAINT.

All weeping eyes resign your tears to me,
   A sea will scantly rinse my ordured soul;
Huge horrors in high tides must drownèd be;
   Of every tear my crime exacteth toll;
These stains are deep, few drops take out no such;
Even salve with sore, and most is not too much.

I fear'd with life to die, by death to live;
   I left my guide,—now left, and leaving God;
To breathe in bliss I fear'd my breath to give,
   I fear'd for heavenly sign an earthly rod;
These fears I fear'd, fears feeling no mishaps,
Oh! fond, oh! faint, oh! false, oh! faulty lapse!

How can I live, that thus my life denied?
   What can I hope, that lost my hope in fear?
What trust in one, that truth itself defied?
   What good in him, that did his God forswear?
O sin of sins! of ills the very worst;
O matchless wretch! O caitiff most accurst!

Vain in my vaunts, I vow'd, if friends had fail'd,
   Alone Christ's hardest fortunes to abide:
Giant in talk, like dwarf in trial quail'd,
   Excelling none but in untruth and pride.
Such distance is between high words and deeds!
In proof, the greatest vaunter seldom speeds.

Ah ! rashness, hasty rise to murdering leap,
  Lavish in vowing, blind in seeing what ;
Soon sowing shames that long remorse must reap,
  Nursing with tears that over-sight begat ;
Scout of repentance, harbinger of blame,
Treason to wisdom, mother of ill name.

The born-blind beggar, for receivèd sight,
  Fast in his faith and love to Christ remain'd ;
He stoopèd to no fear, he fear'd no might,
  No change his choice, no threats his truth distain'd :
One wonder wrought him in his duty sure,
I, after thousands, did my Lord abjure.

Could servile fear of rend'ring Nature's due,
  Which growth in years was shortly like to claim,
So thrall my love, that I should thus eschew
  A vowèd death, and miss so fair an aim ?
Die, die disloyal wretch, thy life detest ;
For saving thine, thou hast forsworn the best.

Ah ! life, sweet drop, drown'd in a sea of sours,
  A flying good, posting to doubtful end ;
Still losing months and years to gain new hours,
  Fain times to have and spare, yet forced to spend ;
Thy growth, decrease ; a moment all thou hast,
That gone ere known ; the rest, to come, or past.

ST. PETER'S COMPLAINT.

Ah! life, the maze of countless straying ways,
    Open to erring steps and strew'd with baits,
To bind weak senses into endless strays,
    Aloof from Virtue's rough, unbeaten straits
A flower, a play, a blast, a shade, a dream,
A living death, a never-turning stream.

And could I rate so high a life so base?
    Did fear with love cast so uneven account,
That for this goal I should run Judas' race,
    And Caiaphas' rage in cruelty surmount?
Yet they esteemèd thirty pence his price;
I, worse than both, for nought denied him thrice.

The mother-sea, from overflowing deep,
    Sends forth her issue by divided veins,
Yet back her offspring to their mother creep,
    To pay the purest streams with added gains.
But I, that drank the drops of heavenly flood,
Bemired the Giver with returning mud!

Is this the harvest of his sowing toil?
    Did Christ manure thy heart to breed him briers?
Or doth it need this unaccustom'd soil,
    With hellish dung to fertile heaven's desires?
No, no, the marl that perjuries do yield,
May spoil a good, not fat a barren field.

Was this for best deserts the direst meed ?
  Are highest worths well waged with spiteful
    hire ?
Are stoutest vows repeal'd in greatest need?
  Should friendship, at the first affront, retire ?
Blush, craven sot, lurk in eternal night ;
Crouched in the darkest cave from loathèd light !

Ah ! wretch, why was I named son of a Dove,
  Whose speeches voided spite and breathèd gall ?
No kin I am unto the bird of love,
  My stony name much better suits my fall :
My oaths were stones, my cruel tongue the sling,
My God the mark at which my spite did fling !

Were all the Jewish tyrannies too few
  To glut thy hungry looks with his disgrace ?
That these more hateful tyrannies must shew,
  And spit thy poison in thy Maker's face ?
Didst thou to spare his foes put up thy sword,
To brandish now thy tongue against thy Lord ?

Ah ! tongue, that didst his praise and Godhead
    sound,
  How wert thou stain'd with such detesting
    words,
That every word was to his heart a wound,
  And lanced him deeper than a thousand swords ?

What rage of man, yea what infernal sprite,
Could have disgorged more loathsome dregs of
spite?

Why did the yielding sea, like marble way,
   Support a wretch more wavering than the waves?
Whom doubt did plunge, why did the waters stay,
   Unkind in kindness, murdering while it saves?
Oh that this tongue had then been fishes' food,
And I devour'd, before this cursing mood!

These surges, depths and seas, unfirm by kind,
   Rough gusts, and distance both from ship and
shore,
Were titles to excuse my staggering mind;
   Stout feet might falter on that liquid floor.
But here no seas, no blasts, no billows were,
   A puff of woman's wind bred all my fear.

O coward troops, far better arm'd than hearted!
   Whom angry words, whom blows could not
provoke;
Whom though I taught how sore my weapon
smarted,
   Yet none repaid me with a wounding stroke.
Oh no! that stroke could but one moiety kill;
I was reserved both halves at once to spill.

Ah! whither was forgotten love exiled;
   Where did the truth of pledgéd promise sleep?

What in my thoughts begat this ugly child,
   That could through rented souls thus fiercely
     creep?
O viper, fear their death by whom thou livest;
All good thy ruins wreck, all ills thou givest!

Threats threw me not, torments I none assay'd;
   My fray with shades; conceits did make me
     yield,
Wounding my thoughts with fears; selfly dismay'd,
   I neither fought nor lost,—I gave the field:
Infamous foil! a maiden's easy breath
Did blow me down, and blast my soul to death.

Titles I make untruths: am I a rock,
   That with so soft a gale was overthrown?
Am I fit pastor for the faithful flock,
   To guide their souls that murder'd thus mine
     own?
A rock of ruin! not a rest to stay;
A pastor,—not to feed, but to betray.

Fidelity was flown when fear was hatch'd,
   Brood incompatible in Virtue's nest!
Courage can less with cowardice be match'd,
   Prowess nor love lodged in divided breast.
O Adam's child, cast by a silly Eve,
Heir to thy father's foils, and born to grieve!

ST. PETER'S COMPLAINT.

In Thabor's joys I eager was to dwell,
    An earnest friend while pleasures' light did
        shine;
But when eclipsèd glory prostrate fell,
    These zealous heats to sleep I did resign;
And now, my mouth hath thrice his name defiled,
That cried so loud three dwellings there to build.

When Christ, attending the distressful hour,
    With His surchargèd breast did bless the ground,
Prostrate in pangs, raining a bleeding shower,
    Me, like myself, a drowsy friend He found.
Thrice, in His care, sleep-closed by careless eye,
Presage how Him my tongue should thrice deny.

Parting from Christ my fainting force declined,
    With lingering foot I follow'd him aloof;
Base fear out of my heart his love unshrined,
    Huge in high words, but impotent in proof.
My vaunts did seem hatch'd under Samson's locks,
Yet woman's words did give me murdering knocks.

So fare lukewarm desires in crazy love,
    Far off, in need, with feeble foot they train;
In tides they swim, low ebbs they scorn to prove;
    They suck their friends' delights, but shun their
        pain.
Hire of an hireling mind is earnèd shame:
Take now thy due, bear thy begotten blame.

Ah! cool remissness, virtue's quartan fever,
　　Pining of love, consumption of grace;
Old in the cradle, languor dying ever,
　　Soul's wilful famine, sin's soft-stealing pace;
The undermining ill of zealous thought,
Seeming to bring no harms, till all be brought!

O portress of the door of my disgrace,
　　Whose tongue unlock'd the truth of vowèd mind;
Whose words from coward's heart did courage chase,
　　And let in deathful fears my soul to blind;
Oh, hadst thou been the portress to my tomb,
When thou wert portress to that cursed room!

Yet love was loath to part, fear loath to die;
　　Stay, danger, life, did counterplead their causes;
I, favouring stay and life, bade danger fly,
　　But danger did except against these clauses:
Yet stay and live I would, and danger shun,
And lost myself, while I my verdict won.

I staid, yet did my staying farthest part;
　　I lived, but so, that saving life I lost it;
Danger I shunn'd, but to my sorer smart,
　　I gainèd nought, but deeper danger crossed it.
What danger, distance, death, is worse than this,
That runs from God and spoils his soul of bliss?

ST. PETER'S COMPLAINT.

O John, my guide unto this earthly hell,
   Too well acquainted in so ill a court,
(Where railing mouths with blasphemies did swell,
   With tainted breath infecting all resort,)
Why didst thou lead me to this hell of evils,
To show myself a fiend among the devils?

Ill precedent, the tide that wafts to vice;
   Dumb orator, that woos with silent deeds,
Writing in works lessons of ill advice;
   The doing tale that eye in practice reads.
Taster of joys to unacquainted hunger,
With leaven of the old seasoning the younger.

It seems no fault to do that all have done;
   The number of offenders hides the sin;
Coach drawn with many horse doth easily run,
   Soon followeth one where multitudes begin.
Oh, had I in that Court much stronger been,
Or not so strong as first to enter in!

Sharp was the weather in that stormy place,
   Best suiting hearts benumb'd with hellish frost,
Whose crusted malice could admit no grace:
   Where coals are kindled to the warmers' cost;
Where fear my thoughts candied with icy cold,
Heat did my tongue to perjuries unfold.

O hateful fire (ah! that I ever saw it)!
  Too hard my heart was frozen for thy force;
Far hotter flames it did require to thaw it,
  Thy hell-resembling heat did freeze it worse.
Oh that I rather had congeal'd to ice,
Than bought thy warmth at such a damning price!

O wakeful bird! proclaimer of the day,
  Whose piercing note doth daunt the lion's rage;
Thy crowing did myself to me bewray,
  My frights and brutish heats it did assuage.
But oh! in this alone, unhappy cock,
That thou to count my foils wert made the clock!

O bird! the just rebuker of my crime,
  The faithful waker of my sleeping fears,
Be now the daily clock to strike the time,
  When stinted eyes shall pay their task of tears;
Upbraid my ears with thine accusing crow,
To make me rue what first it made me know.

O mild revenger of aspiring pride!
  Thou can'st dismount high thoughts to low
    effects;
Thou madest a cock me for my fault to chide,
  My lofty boasts this lowly bird corrects.
Well might a cock correct me with a crow,
Whom hennish cackling first did overthrow.

ST. PETER'S COMPLAINT.

Weak weapons did Goliah's fumes abate,
  Whose storming rage did thunder threats in vain ;
His body huge, harness'd with massy plate,
  Yet David's stone brought death into his brain ;
With staff and sling as to a dog he came,
And with contempt did boasting fury tame.

Yet David had with bear and lion fought,
  His skilful might excused Goliah's foil ;
The death is eased that worthy hand hath wrought;
  Some honour lives in honourable spoil.
But I, on whom all infamies must light,
Was hiss'd to death with words of woman's spite.

Small gnats enforced th' Egyptian King to stoop,
  Yet they in swarms, and arm'd with piercing stings,
Smart, noise, annoyance, made his courage droop ;—
  No small incumbrance such small vermin brings :
I quail'd at words that neither bit nor stung,
And those deliver'd from a woman's tongue.

Ah fear! abortive imp of drooping mind ;
  Self-overthrow, false friend, root of remorse ;
Sighted in seeing ills, in shunning blind,
  Foil'd without field, by fancy not by force ;
Ague of valour, frenzy of the wise,
Fine honour's stain, love's frost, the mint of lies.

Can virtue, wisdom, strength, by woman spill'd
    In David's, Solomon's, and Samson's falls,
With semblance of excuse my error gild,
    Or lend a marble gloss to muddy walls?
O no! their fault had show of some pretence,
No veil can hide the shame of my offence.

The blaze of beauty's beams allured their looks;
    Their looks, by seeing oft, conceivèd love;
Love, by effecting, swallow'd pleasure's hooks;
    Thus beauty, love, and pleasure them did move.
These Syrens' sugar'd tunes rock'd them to sleep,
Enough to damn, yet not to damn so deep.

But gracious features dazzled not mine eyes;
    Two homely droils were authors of my death;
Not love, but fear, my senses did surprise,
    Not fear of force, but fear of woman's breath;
And those unarm'd, ill-graced, despised, unknown:
So base a blast my truth hath overthrown!

O women! woe to men; traps for their falls;
    Still actors in all tragical mischances;
Earth's necessary ills, captiving thralls,
    Now murdering with your tongues, now with your glances;
Parents of life and love, spoilers of both,
The thieves of hearts, false, do you love or loath!

In time, O Lord! thine eyes with mine did meet,
  In them I read the ruins of my fall;
Their cheering rays, that made misfortune sweet,
  Into my guilty thoughts pour'd floods of gall:
Their heavenly looks, that bless'd where they beheld,
Darts of disdain and angry checks did yield.

O sacred eyes! the springs of living light,
  The earthly heavens where angels joy to dwell,
How could you deign to view my deathful plight,
  Or let your heavenly beams look on my hell?
But those unspotted eyes encounter'd mine,
As spotless sun doth on the dunghill shine.

Sweet volumes, stored with learning fit for saints,
  Where blissful quires imparadise their minds;
Wherein eternal study never faints,
  Still finding all, yet seeking all it finds:
How endless is your labyrinth of bliss,
Where to be lost the sweetest finding is!

Ah wretch! how oft have I sweet lessons read
  In those dear eyes, the registers of truth!
How oft have I my hungry wishes fed,
  And in their happy joys redress'd my ruth!
Ah! that they now are heralds of disdain,
That erst were ever pitiers of my pain!

You flames divine, that sparkle out your heats,
  And kindle pleasing fires in mortal hearts;
You nectar'd ambries of soul-feeding meats;
  You graceful quivers of love's dearest darts;
You did vouchsafe to warm, to wound, to feast,
My cold, my stony, my now famish'd breast.

The matchless eyes, match'd only each by other,
  Were pleased on my ill matchèd eyes to glance;
The eye of liquid pearl, the purest mother,
  Broach'd tears in mine to weep for my mischance;
The cabinets of grace unlock'd their treasure,
And did to my misdeed their mercies measure.

These blazing comets, lightning flames of love,
  Made me their warming influence to know;
My frozen heart their sacred force did prove,
  Which at their looks did yield like melting snow:
They did not joys in former plenty carve,
Yet sweet are crumbs where pinèd thoughts do starve.

O living mirrors! seeing whom you show,
  Which equal shadow worths with shadow'd things,
Yea, make things nobler than in native hue,
  By being shaped in those life-giving springs;
Much more my image in those eyes was graced,
Than in myself whom sin and shame defaced!

ST. PETER'S COMPLAINT.

All-seeing eyes, more worth than all you see,
   Of which one is the other's only price;
I worthless am, direct your beams on me,
   With quickening virtue cure my killing vice.
By seeing things you make things worth the sight,
You seeing, salve, and being seen, delight!

Oh! pools of Hesebon, the baths of grace,
   Where happy spirits dive in sweet desires;
Where saints delight to glass their glorious face,
   Whose banks make echo to the angel quires;
An echo sweeter in the sole rebound,
Than angels' music in the fullest sound!

Oh eyes! whose glances are a silent speech,
   In cipher'd works high mysteries disclosing;
Which, with a look, all sciences can teach,
   Whose texts to faithful hearts need little glosing;
Witness unworthy I, who in a look
Learned more by rote, than all the scribes by book!

Though malice still possess'd their harden'd minds,
   I, though too hard, learned softness in thine eye,
Which iron knots of stubborn will unbinds,
   Offering them love, that love with love will buy.
This did I learn, yet they could not discern it;
But woe, that I had now such need to learn it!

O suns ; all but yourselves in light excelling,
　　Whose presence day, whose absence causeth
　　　　night ;
Whose neighbour-course brings Summer, cold
　　　　expelling,
　　Whose distant periods freeze away delight.
Ah ! that I lost your bright and fostering beams,
To plunge my soul in these congealèd streams !

Oh ! gracious spheres, where love the centre is,
　　A native place for our self-laden souls ;
The compass, love,—a cope that none can miss,
　　The motion, love,—that round about us rolls :
Oh ! spheres of love, whose centre, cope and motion,
Is love of us, love that invites devotion !

Oh ! little worlds, the sums of all the best,
　　Whose glory, heaven ; God, sun ; all virtues, stars ;
Whose fire,—a love that next to heaven doth rest ;
　　Air,—light of life that no distemper mars ;
Whose water grace, whose seas, whose springs,
　　　　whose showers,
Clothe Nature's earth with everlasting flowers !

What mixtures these sweet elements do yield,
　　Let happy worldings of these worlds expound ;
But simples are by compounds far excelled,
　　Both suit a place where all best things abound ;
And if a banish'd wretch guess not amiss,
All but one compound frame of perfect bliss.

I, cast-out from these worlds, exiled roam,
    Poor saint from heaven, from fire cold salamander!
Lost fish from those sweet waters' kindly home,
    From land of life stray'd pilgrim still I wander.
I know the cause: these worlds had never hell,
In which my faults have best deserved to dwell.

Oh Bethlem-cisterns! David's most desire,
    From which my sins like fierce Philistines keep;
To fetch your drops what champion should I hire,
    That I therein my wither'd heart may steep?
I would not shed them like that holy king:
His were but types, these are the figured thing.

Oh! turtle twins all bathed in virgin's milk,
    Upon the margin of full-flowing banks,
Whose graceful plume surmounts the finest silk,
    Whose sight enamoureth heaven's most happy ranks:
Could I forswear this heavenly pair of doves,
That caged in care for me were groaning loves!

Twice Moses' hand did strike the stubborn rock,
    Ere stony veins would yield their crystal blood;
Thine eyes, one look, served as an only knock
    To make my heart gush out a weeping flood,
Wherein my sins, as fishes, spawn their fry,
To show their inward shames, and then to die.

But oh! how long demur I on his eyes,
  Whose look did pierce my heart with healing wound!
Lancing imposthumed sore of perjured lies,
  Which these two issues of mine eyes have found;
Where run it must till death the issues stop,
And penal life hath purged the final drop.

Like solest swan, that swims in silent deep,
  And never sings but obsequies of death,
Sigh out thy plaints, and sole in secret weep,
  In suing pardon spend thy perjured breath;
Attire thy soul in sorrow's mourning weed,
And at thine eyes let guilty conscience bleed.

'Still in the 'lembic of thy doleful breast
  Those bitter fruits that from thy sins do grow;
For fuel, self-accusing thoughts be best;
  Use fear as fire, the coals let penance blow;
And seek none other quintessence but tears,
That eyes may shed what enter'd at thine ears.

Come sorrowing tears, the offspring of my grief,
  Scant not your parent of a needful aid;
In you I rest the hope of wish'd relief,
  By you my sinful debts must be defray'd:
Your power prevails, your sacrifice is grateful,
By love obtaining life to men most hateful.

ST. PETER'S COMPLAINT.

Come good effect of ill-deserving cause,
  Ill gotten imps, yet virtuously brought forth ;
Self-blaming probates of infringèd laws,
  Yet blamèd faults redeeming with your worth ;
The signs of shame in you each eye may read,
Yet, while you guilty prove, you pity plead.

O beams of mercy ; beat on sorrow's cloud,
  Pour suppling showers upon my parchèd ground ;
Bring forth the fruit to your due service vow'd,
  Let good desires with like deserts be crown'd :
Water young blooming virtue's tender flow'r,
Sin did all grace of riper growth devour.

Weep balm and myrrh, you sweet Arabian trees,
  With purest gums perfume and pearl your rine ;
Shed on your honey-drops, you busy bees,
  I, barren plant, must weep unpleasant brine :
Hornets I hive, salt drops their labour plies,
Suck'd out of sin, and shed by showering eyes.

If David, night by night, did bathe his bed,
  Esteeming longest days too short to moan ;
Tears inconsolable if Anna shed,
  Who in her son her solace had forgone ;
Then I to days and weeks, to months and years,
Do owe the hourly rent of stintless tears.

If love, if loss, if fault, if spotted fame,
   If danger, death, if wrath, or wreck of weal,
Entitle eyes true heirs to earnèd blame,
   That due remorse in such events conceal :
That want of tears might well enrol my name,
As chiefest saint in kalendar of shame.

Love, where I loved, was due and best deserved ;
   No love could aim at more love-worthy mark ;
No love more loved than mine of him I served ;
   Large use he gave, a flame for every spark.
This love I lost, this loss a life must rue ;
Yea, life is short to pay the ruth is due.

I lost all that I had, who had the most,
   The most that will can wish, or wit devise :
I least perform'd that did most vainly boast,
   I stain'd my fame in most infamous wise.
What danger then, death, wrath, or wreck can move
More pregnant cause of tears than this I prove ?

If Adam sought a veil to scarf his sin,
   Taught by his fall to fear a scourging hand ;
If men shall wish that hills should wrap them in,
   When crimes in final doom come to be scann'd ;
What mount, what cave, what centre can conceal
My monstrous fact, which even the birds reveal ?

ST. PETER'S COMPLAINT.

Come shame, the livery of offending mind,
    The ugly shroud that overshadoweth blame ;
The mulct at which foul faults are justly fined ;
    The damp of sin, the common slime of fame,
By which imposthumed tongues their humours
        purge ;
Light shame on me, I best deserved the scourge.

Cain's murdering hand imbrued in brother's blood,
    More mercy than my impious tongue may crave ;
He kill'd a rival with pretence of good,
    In hope God's doubled love alone to have.
But fear so spoil'd my vanquish'd thoughts of love,
That perjured oaths my spiteful hate did prove.

Poor Agar from her sphere enforced to fly,
    In wilds Barsabian wandering alone,
Doubting her child through helpless drought would
        die,
    Laid it aloof, and set her down to moan :
The heavens with prayers, her lap with tears she
        filled ;
A mother's love in loss is hardly still'd.

But, Agar, now bequeath thy tears to me ;
    Fears, not effects, did set afloat thine eyes.
But, wretch ! I feel more than was fear'd by thee;
    Ah ! not my son, my soul it is that dies.
It dies for drought, yet hath a spring in sight :
Worthy to die, that would not live, and might.

ST. PETER'S COMPLAINT.

Fair Absalom's foul faults compared with mine,
    Are brightest sands to mud of Sodom's lake;
High aims, young spirits, birth of royal line,
    Made him play false where kingdoms were the stake:
He gazed on golden hopes, whose lustre wins,
Sometimes, the gravest wits to grievous sins.

But I, whose crime cuts off the least excuse,
    A kingdom lost, but hoped no mite of gain;
My highest mark was but the worthless use
    Of some few lingering hours of longer pain.
Ungrateful child, his parent he pursued,
I, giants' war with God himself renew'd!

Joy, infant saints, whom in the tender flower
    A happy storm did free from fear of sin!
Long is their life that die in blissful hour;
    Joyful such ends as endless joys begin:
For long they live that live till they be nought:
Life saved by sin, is purchase dearly bought!

This lot was mine; your fate was not so fierce,
    Whom spotless death in cradle rock'd asleep;
Sweet roses, mix'd with lilies, strew'd your hearse,
    Death virgin-white in martyrs' red did steep;
Your downy heads both pearls and rubies crown'd,
My hoary locks did female fears confound.

You bleating ewes, that wail this wolvish spoil
   Of sucking lambs new bought with bitter throes;
To embalm your babes your eyes distil their oil,
   Each heart to tomb her child wide rapture shows.
Rue not their death, whom death did but revive,
Yield ruth to me that lived to die alive.

With easy loss sharp wrecks did he eschew,
   That sindonless aside did naked slip :
Once naked grace no outward garment knew ;
   Such are his robes whom sin did never strip.
I, rich in vaunts, display'd pride's fairest flags,
Disrobed of grace, am wrapp'd in Adam's rags.

When, traitor to the Son, in Mother's eyes
   I shall present my humble suit for grace,
What blush can paint the shame that will arise,
   Or write my inward feelings on my face ?
Might she the sorrow with the sinner see,
Though I'm despised, my grief might pitied be !

But ah ! how can her ears my speech endure,
   Or scent by breath still reeking hellish steam ?
Can Mother like what did the Son abjure,
   Or heart deflower'd a Virgin's love redeem ?
The Mother nothing loves that Son doth loathe :
Ah ! loathsome wretch, detested of them both !

O sister nymphs, the sweet renownèd pair,
   That bless Bethania bounds with your abode !

Shall I infect that sanctifièd air,
  Or stain those steps where Jesus breathed and
    trod?
No, let your prayers perfume that sweeten'd place;
Turn me with tigers to the wildest chace.

Could I revivèd Lazarus behold,
  The third of that sweet trinity of saints,
Would not astonish'd dread my senses hold?
  Ah yes! my heart even with his naming faints:
I seem to see a messenger from hell,
That my preparèd torments comes to tell.

O John! O James! we made a triple cord
  Of three most loving and best lovèd friends;
My rotten twist was broken with a word,
  Fit now to fuel fire among the fiends.
It is not ever true though often spoken,
That triple-twisted cord is hardly broken.

The devils dispossess'd, that out I threw
  In Jusus' name, now impiously forsworn,
Triumph to see me cagèd in their mew,
  Trampling my ruins with contempt and scorn.
My perjuries were music to their dance,
And now they heap disdain on my mischance.

Our rock, say they, is riven; oh, welcome hour
  Our eagle's wings are clipp'd that wrought so
    high;

Our thundering cloud made noise, but cast no
    shower;
  He prostrate lies that would have scaled the sky;
In woman's tongue our rubber found a rub,
Our cedar now is shrunk into a shrub.

These scornful words upbraid my inward thought,
    Proofs of their damnèd prompters' neighbour-
      voice:
Such ugly guests still wait upon the naught,
    Fiends swarm to souls that swerve from virtue's
      choice:
For breach of plighted truth this true I try;
Ah! that my deed thus gave my word the lie!

Once, and but once, too dear a once to twice it!
    A heaven in earth, saints near myself I saw:
Sweet was the sight, but sweeter loves did spice it,
    But sights and loves did my misdeed withdraw.
From heaven and saints, to hell and devils
    estranged,
Those sights to frights, those loves to hates are
    changed.

Christ, as my God, was templed in my thought,
    As man, He lent mine eyes their dearest light;
But sin His temple hath to ruin brought,
    And now he lighteneth terror from His sight.
Now of my late unconsecrate desires,
Profanèd wretch! I taste the earnèd hires.

Ah! sin, the nothing that doth all things file.
  Outcast from heaven, earth's curse, the cause of
    hell;
Parent of death, author of our exile,
  The wreck of souls, the wares that fiends do sell;
That men to monsters, angels turns to devils,
Wrong of all rights, self-ruin, root of evils.

A thing most done, yet more than God can do;
  Daily new done, yet ever done amiss;
Friended of all, yet unto all a foe;
  Seeming an heaven, yet banishing from bliss;
Servèd with toil, yet paying nought but pain,
Man's deepest loss, though false-esteemèd gain.

Shot, without noise; wound, without present smart;
  First seeming light, proving in fine a load;
Entering with ease, not easily won to part,
  Far in effects from that the shows abode;
Indorsed with hope, subscribèd with despair,
Ugly in death, though life did feign it fair.

Oh! forfeiture of heaven! eternal debt,
  A moment's joy ending in endless fires;
Our nature's scum, the world's entangling net,
  Night of our thoughts, death of all good desires.
Worse than all this, worse than all tongues can say,
Which man could owe, but only God defray.

ST. PETER'S COMPLAINT.

This fawning viper, dumb till he had wounded,
    With many mouths doth now upbraid my harms;
My sight was veil'd till I myself confounded,
    Then did I see the disenchanted charms: .
Then could I cut the anatomy of sin,
And search with lynxes' eyes what lay within.

Bewitching ill, that hides death in deceits,
    Still borrowing lying shapes to mask thy face;
Now know I the deciphering of thy sleights;
    A cunning dearly bought with loss of grace:
Thy sugar'd poison now hath wrought so well,
That thou hast made me to myself a hell.

My eyes read mournful lessons to my heart,
    My heart doth to my thought the grief expound;
My thought the same doth to my tongue impart,
    My tongue the message in the ears doth sound;
My ears back to my heart their sorrows send;
Thus circling griefs run round without an end.

My guilty eye still seems to see my sin,
    All things are characters to spell my fall;
What eye doth read without, heart rues within,
    What heart doth rue, to pensive thought is gall,
Which when the thought would by the tongue digest,
The ear conveys it back into the breast.

Thus gripes in all my parts do never fail,
　Whose only league is now in bartering pains;
What I engross they traffic by retail,
　Making each others' miseries their gains:
All bound for ever prentices to care,
Whilst I in shop of shame trade sorrow's ware.

Pleased with displeasing lot I seek no change;
　I wealthiest am when richest in remorse;
To fetch my ware no seas nor lands I range;
　For customers to buy I nothing force:
My home-bred goods at home are bought and sold,
And still in me my interest I hold.

My comfort now is comfortless to live
　In orphan state, devoted to mishap;
But from the root that sweetest fruit did give,
　I scorn'd to graff in stock of meaner sap.
No juice can joy me but of Jesse's flower,
Where heavenly root hath true reviving power.

At Sorrow's door I knock'd, they craved my name:
　I answer'd, one unworthy to be known.
What one? say they. One worthiest of blame.
　But who? a wretch, not God's, nor yet his own.
A man? Oh no! a beast; much worse. What creature?
A rock. How call'd? the rock of scandal, Peter!

ST. PETER'S COMPLAINT.

From whence? From Caiaphas' house. Ah! dwell
   you there?
Sin's farm I rented there, but now would leave it.
What rent? my soul. What gain? unrest and fear.
   Dear purchase! Ah! too dear; will you receive it?
What shall we give? Fit tears and times to plain
   me.
Come in, they say. Thus griefs did entertain me.

With them I rest true prisoner in their jail,
   Chain'd in the iron links of basest thrall;
Till Grace, vouchsafing captive soul to bail,
   In wonted see degraded loves install.
Days pass in plaints, the night without repose;
I wake to sleep; I sleep in waking woes.

Sleep, Death's ally, oblivion of tears,
   Silence of passions, blame of angry sore,
Suspense of loves, security of fears,
   Wrath's lenity, heart's ease, storm's calmest
   shore;
Senses' and souls' reprieval from all cumbers,
Benumbing sense of ill with quiet slumbers.

Not such my sleep, but whisperer of dreams,
   Creating strange chimeras, feigning frights;
Of day-discourses giving fancy themes,
   To make dumb-show with worlds of antic sights;
Casting true griefs in fancy's forgèd mould,
Brokenly telling tales rightly foretold.

This sleep most fitly suiteth sorrow's bed,
 Sorrow, the smart of ill, Sin's eldest child ;
Best, when unkind in killing whom it bred ;
 A rack for guilty thoughts, a bit for wild ;
The scourge that whips, the salve that cures offence ;
Sorrow, my bed and home, while life hath sense.

Here solitary muses nurse their griefs,
 In silent loneness burying worldly noise ;
Attentive to rebukes, deaf to reliefs,
 Pensive to foster cares, careless of joys ;
Ruing life's loss under death's dreary roofs,
Solemnizing my funeral behoofs.

A self-contempt the shroud, my soul the corse,
 The bier, an humble hope, the hearse-cloth, fear ;
The mourners, thoughts, in black of deep remorse,
 The hearse, grace, pity, love and mercy bear :
My tears, my dole, the priest, a zealous will,
Penance, the tomb, and doleful sighs the knell.

Christ ! health of fever'd soul, heaven of the mind,
 Force of the feeble, nurse of infant loves,
Guide to the wandering foot, light to the blind,
 Whom weeping wins, repentant sorrow moves ;
Father in care, mother in tender heart,
Revive and save me, slain with sinful dart.

ST. PETER'S COMPLAINT.

If King Manasses, sunk in depth of sin,
   With plaints and tears recover'd grace and crown,
A worthless worm some mild regard may win,
   And lowly creep, where flying threw it down.
A poor desire I have to mend my ill,
I should, I would, I dare not say, I will.

I dare not say I will, but wish I may;
   My pride is check'd, high words the speaker spilt.
My good, O Lord! Thy gift, Thy strength mistay,
   Give what Thou bidst, and then bid what Thou wilt.
Work with me what of me thou dost request,
Then will I dare the worst and love the best.

Prone look, cross'd arms, bent knee and contrite heart,
   Deep sighs, thick sobs, dew'd eyes and prostrate pray'rs,
Most humbly beg release of earnèd smart,
   And saving shroud in mercy's sweet repairs.
If justice should my wrongs with rigour wage,
Fears would despairs, ruth breed a hopeless rage.

Lazar at pity's gate I ulcer'd lie,
   Craving the refuse crumbs of children's plate;
My sores I lay in view to Mercy's eye,
   My rags bear witness of my poor estate:

The worms of conscience that within me swarm,
Prove that my plaints are less than is my harm.

With mildness, Jesu, measure mine offence;
　Let true remorse Thy due revenge abate;
Let tears appease when trespass doth increase;
　Let pity temper Thy deservèd hate;
Let grace forgive, let love forget my fall:
With fear I crave, with hope I humbly call.

Redeem my lapse with ransom of Thy love,
　Traverse th' indictment, rigour's doom suspend;
Let frailty favour, sorrows succour move,
　Be Thou Thyself, though changeling I offend.
Tender my suit, cleanse this defilèd den,
Cancel my debts, sweet Jesu, say Amen!

MARY MAGDALEN'S BLUSH.

THE signs of shame that stain my blushing face
  Rise from the feeling of my raving fits,
Whose joy annoy, whose guerdon is disgrace,
Whose solace flies, whose sorrow never flits;
Bad seed I sow'd, worse seed is now my gain,
Soon-dying mirth begat long-living pain.

Now pleasure ebbs, revenge begins to flow;
One day doth work the wrath that many wrought;
Remorse doth teach my guilty thoughts to know
How cheap I sold that Christ so dearly bought:
Faults long unfelt doth conscience now bewray,
Which cares must cure and tears must wash away.

All ghostly dints that grace at me did dart,
Like stubborn rock I forcèd to recoil;
To other flights an aim I made my heart
Whose wounds, then welcome, now have wrought
    my foil.
Woe worth the bow, woe worth the archer's might,
That draw such arrows to the mark so right!

To pull them out, to leave them in is death,
One to this world, one to the world to come;
Wounds may I wear and draw a doubtful breath,
But then my wounds will work a dreadful doom;
And for a world whose pleasures pass away,
I lose a world whose joys are past decay.

O sense! O soul! O hap! O hopèd bliss!
You woo, you win, you draw, you drive me back;
Your cross encount'ring like their combat is,
That never end but with some deadly wrack;
When sense doth win, the soul doth lose the field,
And present haps make future hopes to yield.

O heaven! lament, sense robbeth thee of saints,
Lament, O souls! sense spoileth you of grace;
Yet sense doth scarce deserve these hard complaints,
Love is the chief, sense but the entering place;
Yet grant I must, sense is not free from sin,
For thief he is that thief admitteth in.

MARY MAGDALEN'S COMPLAINT AT CHRIST'S DEATH.

SITH my life from life is parted,
 Death come take thy portion,
 Who survives when life is murder'd
Lives by mere extortion:
All that live and not in God,
Couch their life in death's abode.

Silly stars must needs leave shining
 When the sun is shadowèd,
Borrow'd streams refrain their running
 When head springs are hinderèd:
One that lives by other's breath,
Dieth also by his death.

O true life! sith Thou hast left me,
 Mortal life is tedious;
Death it is to live without Thee,
 Death of all most odious:
Turn again or take me to Thee,
Let me die or live Thou in me!

MARY MAGDALEN'S COMPLAINT.

> Where the truth once was and is not,
>   Shadows are but vanity;
> Showing want that help they cannot,
>   Signs, not salves, of misery.
> Painted meat no hunger feeds,
> Dying life each death exceeds.
>
> With my love my life was nestled
>   In the sun of happiness;
> From my love my life is wrested
>   To a world of heaviness:
> Oh! let love my life remove,
> Sith I live not where I love!
>
> O my soul! that did unloose thee
>   From thy sweet captivity,
> God, not I, did still possess thee,
>   His, not mine, thy liberty:
> Oh! too happy thrall thou wert,
> When thy prison was his heart.
>
> Spiteful spear that break'st this prison,
>   Seat of all felicity,
> Working thus with double treason
>   Love's and life's delivery:
> Though my life thou draw'st away,
> Maugre thee my love shall stay.

TIMES GO BY TURNS.

THE loppèd tree in time may grow again;
  Most naked plants renew both fruit and
      flower;
The sorest wight may find release of pain,
The driest soil suck in some moistening shower;
Times go by turns and chances change by course,
From foul to fair, from better hap to worse.

The sea of Fortune doth not ever flow,
She draws her favours to the lowest ebb;
Her time hath equal times to come and go,
Her loom doth weave the fine and coarsest web;
No joy so great but runneth to an end,
No hap so hard but may in fine amend.

Not always fall of leaf nor ever spring,
No endless night yet not eternal day;
The saddest birds a season find to sing,
The roughest storm a calm may soon allay;
Thus with succeeding turns God tempereth all,
That man may hope to rise yet fear to fall.

A chance may win that by mischance was lost;
The well that holds no great, takes little fish;
In some things all, in all things none are cross'd,
Few all they need, but none have all they wish;
Unmeddled joys here to no man befall,
Who least hath some, who most hath never all.

LOOK HOME.

RETIRED thoughts enjoy their own delights,
  As beauty doth in self-beholding eye;
  Man's mind a mirror is of heavenly sights,
A brief wherein all marvels summèd lie,
Of fairest forms and sweetest shapes the store,
Most graceful all, yet thought may grace them
    more.

The mind a creature is, yet can create,
To nature's patterns adding higher skill;
Of finest works wit better could the state
If force of wit had equal power of will:
Device of man in working hath no end;
What thought can think another thought can
    mend.

Man's soul of endless beauties image is,
Drawn by the work of endless skill and might;
This skilful might gave many sparks of bliss,
And to discern this bliss a native light;
To frame God's image as His worths required,
His might, His skill, His word and will conspired.

All that he had His image should present,
All that it should present he could afford,
To that he could afford his will was bent,
This will was follow'd with performing word;
Let this suffice, by this conceive the rest,
He should, he could, he would, he did the best.

FORTUNE'S FALSEHOOD.

IN worldly merriments lurketh much misery,
Fly fortune's subtleties in baits of happiness;
Shroud hooks that swallowèd without recovery,
Murder the innocent with mortal heaviness.

She sootheth appetites with pleasing vanities,
Till they be conquerèd with cloakèd tyranny;
Then changing countenance with open enmities,
She triumphs over them, scorning their slavery.

With fawning flattery death's door she openeth,
Alluring passengers to bloody destiny;
In offers bountiful in proof she beggareth,
Man's ruins regist'ring her false felicity.

Her hopes are fastenèd in bliss that vanisheth,
Her smarts inherited with sure possession;
Constant in cruelty she never altereth,
But from one violence to more oppression.

To those that follow her favours are measurèd,
As easy premises to hard conclusions;

With bitter corrosives her joys are seasonèd,
Her highest benefits are but illusions.

Her ways a labyrinth of wand'ring passages,
Fools' common pilgrimage to cursèd deities;
Whose fond devotion and idle menages
Are waged with weariness in fruitless drudgeries.

Blind in her favourites' foolish election,
Chance in her arbiter in giving dignities,
Her choice of vicious shows most discretion,
Sith wealth the virtuous might wrest from piety.

To humble suppliants tyrant most obstinate,
She suitors answereth with contrarieties;
Proud with petition, untaught to mitigate
Rigour with clemency in hardest cruelties.

Like tiger fugitive from the ambitions,
Like weeping crocodile to scornful enemies,
Suing for amity where she is odious,
But to her followers forswearing courtesies.

No wind so changeable, no sea so wavering,
As giddy fortune in reeling vanities;
Now mad, now merciful, now fierce, now favouring,
In all things mutable but mutabilities.

SCORN NOT THE LEAST.

WHERE wards are weak and foes encount-
    'ring strong,
Where mightier do assault than do defend,
The feebler part puts up enforcèd wrong,
And silent sees that speech could not amend.
Yet higher powers must think though they repine,
When sun is set, the little stars will shine.

While pike doth range the silly tench doth fly,
And crouch in privy creeks with smaller fish;
Yet pikes are caught when little fish go by,
These fleet afloat while those do fill the dish.
There is a time even for the worms to creep,
And suck the dew while all their foes do sleep.

The martin cannot ever soar on high,
Nor greedy greyhound still pursue the chase;
The tender lark will find a time to fly,
And fearful hare to run a quiet race.
He that the growth on cedars did bestow,
Gave also lowly mushrooms leave to grow.

SCORN NOT THE LEAST.

In Aman's pomp poor Mardocheus wept,
Yet God did turn his fate upon his foe;
The Lazar pined while Dives' feast was kept,
Yet he to heaven, to hell did Dives go.
We trample grass and prize the flowers of May,
Yet grass is green when flowers do fade away.

A CHILD MY CHOICE.

LET folly praise that fancy loves,
    I praise and love that child
Whose heart no thought, whose tongue no word,
    Whose head no deed defiled;

I praise him most, I love him best,
    All praise and love is his;
While him I love, in him I live,
    And cannot live amiss.

Love's sweetest mark, land's highest theme,
    Man's most desirèd light,
To love him life, to leave him death,
    To live in him delight.

He mine by gift, I him by debt,
    Thus each to other due,
First friend he was, best friend he is,
    All times will try him true.

A CHILD MY CHOICE.

Though young, yet wise; though small, yet
    strong;
Though man, yet God he is;
As wise he knows, as strong he can,
    As God he loves to bless.

His knowledge rules, his strength defends,
    His love doth cherish all;
His birth our joy, his life our light,
    His death our end of thrall.

Alas! he weeps, he sighs, he pants,
    Yet doth his angels sing;
Out of his tears, his sighs and throbs,
    Doth bud a joyful spring.

Almighty babe, whose tender arms
    Can force all foes to fly,
Correct my faults, protect my life,
    Direct me when I die!

CONTENT AND RICH.

I DWELL in Grace's court,
   Enrich'd with Virtue's rights;
Faith guides my wit, Love leads my will,
   Hope all my mind delights.

In lowly vales I mount
   To pleasure's highest pitch;
My silly shroud true honour brings,
   My poor estate to rich.

My conscience is my crown,
   Contented thoughts my rest;
My heart is happy in itself,
   My bliss is in my breast.

Enough I reckon wealth;
   A mean the surest lot,
That lies too high for base contempt,
   Too low for envy's shot.

My wishes are but few,
   All easy to fulfil,
I make the limits of my power
   The bounds unto my will.

CONTENT AND RICH.

I have no hope but one,
  Which is of heavenly reign;
Effects attend, or not desire,
  All lower hopes refrain.

I feel no care of coin,
  Well-doing is my wealth;
My mind to me an empire is,
  While grace affordeth health.

I clip high-climbing thoughts,
  The wings of swelling pride;
Their fall is worst, that from the height,
  Of greatest honours slide.

Sith sails of largest size
  The storm doth soonest tear,
I bear so low and small a sail
  As freeth me from fear.

I wrestle not with rage,
  While fury's flame doth burn;
It is in vain to stop the streams
  Until the tide doth turn.

But when the flame is out,
  And ebbing wrath doth end,
I turn a late enlargèd foe
  Into a quiet friend.

CONTENT AND RICH.

And taught with often proof,
   A temper'd calm I find
To be most solace to itself,
   Best cure for angry mind.

Spare diet is my fare,
   My clothes more fit than fine;
I know I feed and clothe a foe
   That pamper'd would repine.

I envy not their hap,
   Whom favour doth advance;
I take no pleasure in their pain,
   That have less happy chance.

To rise by others' fall
   I deem a losing gain;
All states with others' ruins built,
   To ruin run amain.

No chance of Fortune's calms
   Can cast my comforts down;
When fortune smiles, I smile to think
   How quickly she will frown.

And when in froward mood
   She proves an angry foe,
Small gain I found to let her come,
   Less loss to let her go.

LOSS IN DELAY.

SHUN delays, they breed remorse;
    Take thy time while time is lent thee;
Creeping snails have weakest force,
    Fly their fault lest thou repent thee.
Good is best when soonest wrought,
Linger'd labours come to nought.

Hoist up sail while gale doth last,
    Tide and wind stay no man's pleasure;
Seek not time when time is past,
    Sober speed is wisdom's leisure.
After-wits are dearly bought,
Let thy forewit guide thy thought.

Time wears all his locks before,
    Take thy hold upon his forehead;
When he flies he turns no more,
    And behind his scalp is naked.
Works adjourn'd have many stays;
Long demurs breed new delays.

LOSS IN DELAY.

Seek thy salve while sore is green,
    Fester'd wounds ask deeper lancing;
After-cures are seldom seen,
    Often sought scarce ever chancing.
Time and place give best advice,
Out of season, out of price.

Crush the serpent in the head,
    Break ill eggs ere they be hatch'd;
Kill bad chickens in the tread,
    Fledged, they hardly can be catch'd.
In the rising stifle ill,
Lest it grow against thy will.

Drops do pierce the stubborn flint,
    Not by force but often falling;
Custom kills with feeble dint,
    More by use than strength and vailing.
Single sands have little weight,
Many make a drawing freight.

Tender twigs are bent with ease,
    Aged trees do break with bending;
Young desires make little prease,
    Growth doth make them past amending.
Happy man, that soon doth knock
Babel's babes against the rock!

LOVE'S SERVILE LOT.

LOVE mistress is of many minds,
    Yet few know whom they serve;
They reckon least how little love
    Their service doth deserve.

The will she robbeth from the wit,
    The sense from reason's lore;
She is delightful in the rind,
    Corrupted in the core.

She shroudeth vice in virtue's veil,
    Pretending good in ill;
She offereth joy, affordeth grief,
    A kiss, where she doth kill.

A honey-shower rains from her lips,
    Sweet lights shine in her face;
She hath the blush of virgin's mind,
    The mind of viper's race.

She makes thee seek, yet fear to find;
    To find but not enjoy;
In many frowns some gliding smiles,
    She yields, to more annoy.

LOVE'S SERVILE LOT.

She woos thee to come near her fire,
    Yet doth draw it from thee;
Far off she makes thy heart to fry,
    And yet to freeze in thee.

She letteth fall some luring baits,
    For fools to gather up;
To sweet, to sour, to every taste
    She tempereth her cup.

Soft souls she binds in tender twist,
    Small flies in spinner's web;
She sets afloat some luring streams,
    But makes them soon to ebb.

Her watery eyes have burning force,
    Her floods and flames conspire;
Tears kindle sparks, sobs fuel are,
    And sighs do blow her fire.

May never was the month of love,
    For May is full of flowers;
But rather April, wet by kind,
    For love is full of showers.

Like tyrant, cruel wounds she gives,
    Like surgeon, salves she lends;
But salve and sore have equal force,
    For death is both their ends.

With soothèd words enthrallèd souls
    She chains in servile bands;
Her eye in silence hath a speech,
    Which eye best understands.

Her little sweet hath many sours;
    Short hap immortal harms;
Her loving looks are murdering darts,
    Her songs, bewitching charms.

Like winter rose and summer ice,
    Her joys are still untimely;
Before her hope, behind remorse,
    Fair first, in fine unseemly.

Moods, passions, fancies, jealous fits,
    Attend upon her train;
She yieldeth rest without repose,
    A heaven in hellish pain.

Her house is sloth, her door deceit,
    And slippery hope her stairs;
Unbashful boldness bids her guests,
    And every vice repairs.

Her diet is of such delights
    As please, till they be past;
But then, the poison kills the heart
    That did entice the taste.

LOVE'S SERVILE LOT.

Her sleep in sin doth end in wrath,
    Remorse rings her awake;
Death calls her up, shame drives her out,
    Despairs her upshot make.

Plough not the seas, sow not the sands,
    Leave off your idle pain;
Seek other mistress for your minds,
    Love's service is in vain.

LIFE IS BUT LOSS.

BY force I live, in will I wish to die;
   In plaints I pass the length of ling'ring
      days;
Free would my soul from mortal body fly,
   And tread the track of death's desirèd ways:
Life is but loss where death is deemèd gain,
And loathèd pleasures breed displeasing pain.

Who would not die to kill all murd'ring grieves?
   Or who would live in never-dying fears?
Who would not wish his treasure safe from thieves,
   And quit his heart from pangs, his eyes from
      tears?
Death parteth but two ever-fighting foes,
Whose civil strife doth work our endless woes.

Life is a wandering course to doubtful rest;
   As oft a cursèd rise to damning leap,
As happy race to win a heavenly crest;
   None being sure what final fruits to reap:
And who can like in such a life to dwell,
Whose ways are strict to heaven, but wide to hell?

LIFE IS BUT LOSS.

Come, cruel death, why lingerest thou so long?
　　What doth withhold thy dint from fatal stroke?
Now prest I am, alas! thou dost me wrong,
　　To let me live more anger to provoke:
Thy right is had when thou hast stopp'd my breath,
Why shouldst thou stay to work my double death?

If Saul's attempt in falling on his blade
　　As lawful were as eth to put in ure,
If Samson's lean a common law were made,
　　Of Abel's lot if all that would were sure,
Then, cruel death, thou shouldst the tyrant play
With none but such as wishèd for delay.

Where life is loved thou ready art to kill,
　　And to abridge with sudden pangs their joys;
Where life is loathed thou wilt not work their will,
　　But dost adjourn their death to their annoy.
To some thou art a fierce unbidden guest,
But those that crave thy help thou helpest least.

Avaunt, O viper! I thy spite defy:
　　There is a God that overrules thy force,
Who can thy weapons to His will apply,
　　And shorten or prolong our brittle course.
I on His mercy, not thy might, rely;
To Him I live, for Him I hope to die.

I DIE ALIVE.

 LIFE! what lets thee from a quick decease?
    O death! what draws thee from a present
      prey?
My feast is done, my soul would be at ease,
    My grace is said, O death! come take away.

I live, but such a life as ever dies;
    I die, but such a death as never ends;
My death to end my dying life denies,
    And life my loving death no whit amends.

Thus still I die, yet still I do remain;
    My living death by dying life is fed;
Grace more than nature keeps my heart alive,
    Whose idle hopes and vain desires are dead.

Not where I breathe, but where I love, I live;
    Not where I love, but where I am, I die;
The life I wish must future glory give,
    The death I feel in present dangers lie.

WHAT JOY TO LIVE.

I WAGE no war, yet peace I none enjoy;
   I hope, I fear, I fry in freezing cold;
   I mount in mirth, still prostrate in annoy;
If all the world embrace yet nothing hold.
All wealth is want where chiefest wishes fail,
Yea life is loathed where love may not prevail.

For that I love I long, but that I lack;
   That other love I loath, and that I have;
All worldly freights to me are deadly wrack,
   Men present hap, I future hopes do crave:
They, loving where they live, long life require,
To live where best I love, I death desire.

Here loan is lent for love of filthy gain;
   Most friends befriend themselves with friendship's show;
Here plenty peril, want doth breed disdain;
   Cares common are, joys faulty, short and few;
Here honour envied, meanness is despised;
   Sin deemèd solace, virtue little prized.

Here beauty is a bait that, swallow'd, chokes;
A treasure sought still in the owner's harms ;
A light that eyes to murdering sights provokes,
A grace that souls enchants with mortal charms;
A luring gain to Cupid's fiery slights,
A baleful bliss that damns where it delights.

Oh! who would live so many deaths to try?
Where will doth wish that wisdom doth reprove,
Where nature craves that grace must needs deny,
Where sense doth like that reason cannot love,
Where best in show in final proof is worst,
Where pleasures upshot is to die accurst?

LIFE'S DEATH, LOVE'S LIFE.

WHO lives in love, loves least to live,
    And long delays doth rue,
If Him he love by whom he lives,
    To whom all love is due.

Who for our love did choose to live,
    And was content to die;
Who loved our love more than His life,
    And love with life did buy.

Let us in life, yea with our life,
    Requite His living love;
For best we live when best we love,
    If love our life remove.

Where love is hot life hateful is,
    Their grounds do not agree;
Love where it loves, life where it lives,
    Desireth most to be.

And sith love is not where it lives,
    Nor liveth where it loves,
Love hateth life that holds it back,
    And death it best approves.

LIFE'S DEATH, LOVE'S LIFE.

For seldom is He won in life
   Whom love doth most desire;
If won in love, yet not enjoy'd,
   Till mortal life expire.

Life out of earth hath no abode,
   In earth love hath no place;
Love settled hath her joys in heaven,
   In earth life all her grace.

Mourn, therefore, no true lover's death,
   Life only him annoys;
And when he taketh leave of life,
   Then love begins his joys.

AT HOME IN HEAVEN.

FAIR soul! how long shall veils thy graces
    shroud?
  How long shall this exile withhold thy right?
When will thy sun disperse his mortal cloud,
    And give thy glories scope to blaze their light?
Oh that a star, more fit for angel's eyes,
Should pine in earth, not shine above the skies!

Thy ghostly beauty offer'd force to God;
    It chainèd Him in links of tender love;
It won His will with man to make abode;
    It stay'd His sword, and did His wrath remove:
It made the vigour of His justice yield,
And crownèd Mercy empress of the field.

This lull'd our heavenly Samson fast asleep,
    And laid Him in our feeble nature's lap;
This made Him under mortal load to creep,
    And in our flesh His Godhead to enwrap;
This made Him sojourn with us in exile,
And not disdain our titles in His style.

This brought Him from the ranks of heavenly
    quires
    Into this vale of tears and cursèd soil ;
From flowers of grace into a world of briars,
    From life to death, from bliss to baleful toil.
This made Him wander in our pilgrim weed,
And taste our torments to relieve our need.

O soul! do not thy noble thoughts abase,
    To lose thy loves in any mortal wight ;
Content thy eye at home with native grace,
    Sith God Himself is ravish'd with thy sight :
If on thy beauty God enamoured be,
Base is thy love of any less than He.

Give not assent to muddy-minded skill,
    That deems the feature of a pleasing face
To be the sweetest bait to lure the will ;
    Not valuing right the worth of ghostly grace ;
Let God's and angels' censure win belief,
That of all beauties judge our souls the chief.

Queen Hester was of rare and peerless hue,
    And Judith once for beauty bare the vaunt ;
But he that could our souls' endowments view,
    Would soon to souls the crown of beauty grant.
O soul ! out of thyself seek God alone :
Grace more than thine, but God's, the world hath
    none.

LEWD LOVE IS LOSS.

MISDEEMING eye! that stoopest to the lure
    Of mortal worths, not worth so worthy
       love;
All beauties base, all graces are impure,
    That do thy erring thoughts from God remove.
Sparks to the fire, the beams yield to the sun,
All grace to God, from whom all graces run.

If picture move, more should the pattern please;
    No shadow can with shadow'd thing compare,
And fairest shapes, whereon our loves do seize,
    But folly signs of God's high beauty are.
Go, starving sense, feed thou on earthly mast;
True love is heaven, seek thou thy sweet repast.

Glean not in barren soil these offal ears,
    Sith reap thou may'st whole harvests of delight;
Base joys in griefs, bad hopes do end in fears,
    Lewd love in loss, evil peace in deadly fight:
God's love alone doth end in endless ease,
Whose joys in hope, whose hope concludes in peace.

LEWD LOVE IS LOSS.

Let not the luring train of fancy's trap,
    Or gracious features, proofs of Nature's skill,
Lull Reason's force asleep in Error's lap,
    Or draw thy wit to bent of wanton will.
The fairest flowers have not the sweetest smell;
A seeming heaven proves oft a damning hell.

Self-pleasing souls, that play with beauty's bait,
    In shining shroud may swallow fatal hook;
Where eager sight on semblant fair doth wait,
    A lock it proves, that first was but a look:
The fish with ease into the net doth glide,
But to get out the way is not so wide.

So long the fly doth dally with the flame,
    Until his singèd wings do force his fall;
So long the eye doth follow fancy's game,
    Till love hath left the heart in heavy thrall.
Soon may the mind be cast in Cupid's jail,
But hard it is imprison'd thoughts to bail.

Oh! loathe that love whose final aim is lust,
    Moth of the mind, eclipse of reason's light;
The grave of grace, the mole of Nature's rust,
    The wrack of wit, the wrong of every right.
In sum, an ill whose harms no tongue can tell;
In which to live is death, to die is hell.

LOVE'S GARDEN GRIEF.

VAIN loves, avaunt! infamous is your pleasure,
  Your joys deceit;
 Your jewels jests, and worthless trash your
   treasure,
 Fools' common bait.
Your palace is a prison that allureth
To sweet mishap, and rest that pain procureth.

Your garden grief hedged in with thorns of envy
  And stakes of strife;
Your allies error gravel'd with jealousy
  And cares of life;
Your branches seats enwrapp'd with shades of
   sadness;
Your arbours breed rough fits of raging madness.

Your beds are sown with seeds of all iniquity
  And poisoning weeds,
Whose stalks ill thoughts, whose leaves words full
   of vanity,
  Whose fruits misdeeds;
Whose sap is sin, whose force and operation,
To banish grace and work the soul's damnation.

Your trees are dismal plants of pining corrosives,
    Whose root is ruth,
Whose bark is bale, whose timber stubborn fantasies,
    Whose pith untruth;
On which in lieu of birds whose voice delighteth,
Of guilty conscience screeching note affrighteth.

Your coolest summer gales are scalding sighings,
    Your showers are tears;
Your sweetest smell the stench of sinful living,
    Your favours fears;
Your gard'ner Satan, all you reap is misery,
Your gain remorse and loss of all felicity.

FROM FORTUNE'S REACH.

LET fickle Fortune run her blindest race,
    I settled have an unremovèd mind;
      I scorn to be [the] game of Fancy's chase,
    Or vane to show the change of every wind.
Light giddy humours, stinted in no rest,
Still change their choice, yet never choose the best.

My choice was guided by foresightful heed,
    It was averrèd with approving will;
It shall be follow'd with performing deed,
    And seal'd with vow, till death the chooser kill.
Yet death, though final date of vain desires,
Ends not my choice, which with no time expires.

To beauty's fading bliss I am no thrall;
    I bury not my thoughts in metal mines;
I aim not at such fame as feareth fall;
    I seek and find a light that ever shines:
Whose glorious beams display such heavenly sights,
As yield my soul the sum of all delights.

My light to love, my love to light doth guide,—
　　To life that lives by love, and loveth light;
By love to one, to whom all loves are tied
　　By duest debt, and never equall'd right;
Eyes' light, heart's love, soul's truest life He is,
Consorting in three joys one perfect bliss.

A FANCY TURNED TO A SINNER'S COMPLAINT.*

HE that his mirth hath lost,
    Whose comfort is to rue;
Whose hope is salve, whose faith is crazed,
    Whose trust is found untrue;

If he have held them dear,
    And cannot cease to moan,
Come let him take his place by me,
    He shall not rue alone.

But if the smallest sweet
    Be mix'd with all his sour;
If in the day, the month, the year,
    He feel one lighting hour;

Then rest he with himself,
    He is no mate for me,
Whose time in tears, whose race in ruth,
    Whose life in death must be.

* In MS. "Master Dier's Fancy turned to a Sinner's Complaint."

Yet not the wishèd death,
   That feels in plaint or lack,
That making free the better part
   Is only nature's wrack.

Oh no! that were too well;
   My death is of the mind,
That always yields extremest pangs,
   Yet threatens worse behind.

As one that lives in show,
   And inwardly doth die,
Whose knowledge is a bloody field,
   Where virtue slain doth lie;

Whose heart the altar is,
   And host a God to move,
From whom my evil fears revenge,
   His good doth promise love.

My fancies are like thorns
   In which I go by night;
My frighted wits are like a host
   That force hath put to flight.

My sense is passion's spy,
   My thoughts like ruins old,
Which show how fair the building was
   While grace did it uphold.

A SINNER'S COMPLAINT.

And still before mine eyes
    My mortal fall they lay;
Whom grace and virtue once advanced,
    Now sin hath cast away.

Oh thoughts! no thoughts but wounds,
    Sometime the seat of joy,
Sometimes the store of quiet rest,
    But now of all annoy.

I sow'd the soil of peace,
    My bliss was in the spring;
And day by day the fruit I eat
    That virtue's tree did bring.

To nettles now my corn,
    My field is turned to flint,
Where I a heavy harvest reap
    Of cares that never stint.

The peace, the rest, the life,
    That I enjoy'd of yore,
Were happy lot, but by their loss
    My smart doth sting the more.

So to unhappy men,
    The best frames to the worst;
Oh time! oh place! where thus I fell;
    Dear then, but now accurst.

In was stands my delight,
   In is and shall my woe;
My horror fasten'd in the yea,
   My hope hang'd in the no.

Unworthy of relief,
   That cravèd it too late,
Too late I find, I find too well,
   Too well stood my estate.

Behold, such is the end
   That pleasure doth procure,
Of nothing else but care and plaint
   Can she the mind assure.

Forsaken first by grace,
   By pleasure now forgotten;
Her pain I feel, but grace's wage
   Have others from me gotten.

Then grace where is the joy
   That makes thy torments sweet?
Where is the cause that many thought
   Their deaths through thee but meet?

Where thy disdain of sin,
   Thy secret sweet delight?
Thy sparks of bliss, thy heavenly rays,
   That shinèd erst so bright?

A SINNER'S COMPLAINT.

Oh! that they were not lost,
   Or I could it excuse;
Oh! that a dream of feignèd loss
   My judgment did abuse!

O frail inconstant flesh!
   Soon wrapt in every gin,
Soon wrought thus to betray thy soul,
   And plunge thyself in sin.

Yet have I but the fault,
   And not the faulty one,
Nor can I rid from me the mate
   That forceth me to moan.

To moan a sinner's case,
   Than which was never worse,
In prince or poor, in young or old,
   In bliss or full of curse.

Yet God's must I remain,
   By death, by wrong, by shame;
I cannot blot out of my heart
   That grace wrought in His name.

I cannot set at nought
   Whom I have held so dear;
I cannot make Him seem afar
   That is indeed so near.

Not that I look henceforth
  For love that erst I found ;
Sith that I brake my plighted troth
  To build on fickle ground.

Yet that shall never fail
  Which my faith has in hand ;
I gave my vow, my vow gave me,
  Both vow and gift shall stand.

But since that I have sinn'd,
  And scourge none is too ill,
I yield me captive to my curse,
  My hard fate to fulfil.

The solitary wood
  My city shall become ;
The darkest dens shall be my lodge,
  In which I rest or come.

A sandy plot my board,
  The worms my feast shall be,
Wherewith my carcase shall be fed,
  Until they feed on me.

My tears shall be my wine,
  My bed a craggy rock ;
My harmony the serpent's hiss,
  The screeching owl my clock.

A SINNER'S COMPLAINT.

My exercise, remorse
    And doleful sinners' lays;
My book, remembrance of my crimes,
    And faults of former days.

My walk, the path of plaint,
    My prospect into hell
Where Judas and his cursèd crew
    In endless pain do dwell.

And though I seem to use
    The feigning poets style,
To figure forth my careful plight,
    My fall and my exile.

Yet is my grief not feign'd,
    Wherein I starve and pine;
Who feeleth most shall think it least,
    If his compare with mine.

DAVID'S PECCAVI.*

IN eaves sole sparrow sits not more alone,
   Nor mourning pelican in desert wild,
  Than silly I that solitary moan,
  From highest hopes to hardest hap exiled:
Sometime, oh, blissful time! was virtue's meed
Aim to my thoughts, guide to my word and deed.

But fears now are my feres, grief my delight,
   My tears my drink, my famish'd thoughts my bread;
Day full of dumps, nurse of unrest the night,
   My garments give a bloody field my bed;
My sleep is rather death than death's ally,
Yet kill'd with murdering pangs I cannot die.

This is the change of my ill chargèd choice,
   Ruth for my rest, for comforts care I find;
To pleasing tunes succeed a plaining voice,
   The doleful echo of my wailing mind;
Which, taught to know the worth of virtue's joys,
Doth hate itself, for loving fancy's toys.

      * In Douay Edition, "St. Peter's."

DAVID'S PECCAVI.

If wiles of wit had overwrought my will,
    Or subtle trains misled my steps away,
My foil had found excuse in want of skill,
    Ill deed I might, though not ill doom deny.
But wit and will must now confess with shame,
Both deed and doom to have deservèd blame.

In fancy, deem'd fit guide to lead my way,
    And as I deem'd I did pursue her track,
Wit lost his aim and will was fancy's prey;
    The rebel won, the ruler went to wrack.
But now sith fancy did with folly end,
Wit bought with loss, will taught by wit will mend.

SIN'S HEAVY LOAD.

LORD! my sins doth overcharge thy breast,
    The poise thereof doth force thy knees to bow;
Yea, flat thou fallest with my faults oppress'd,
    And bloody sweat runs trickling from thy brow:
But had they not to earth thus pressèd thee,
Much more they would in hell have pester'd me.

This globe of earth doth thy one finger prop,
    The world thou dost within thy hand embrace;
Yet all this weight of sweat drew not a drop,
    Nor made thee bow, much less fall on thy face;
But now thou hast a load so heavy found,
That makes thee bow, yea fall flat to the ground.

O Sin! how huge and heavy is thy weight,
    That weighest more than all the world beside;
Of which when Christ had taken in His freight,
    The poise thereof His flesh could not abide.
Alas! if God Himself sink under sin,
What will become of man that dies therein?

SIN'S HEAVY LOAD.

First flat thou fell'st where earth did thee receive,
   In closet pure of Mary's virgin breast;
And now thou fall'st of earth to take thy leave,
   Thou kissest it as cause of thy unrest:
O loving Lord! that so dost love thy foe
As thus to kiss the ground where he doth go.

Thou, minded in thy heaven our earth to wear,
   Doth prostrate now thy heaven our earth to
     bless;
As God to earth thou often wert severe,
   As man thou seal'st a peace with bleeding kiss:
For as of souls thou common father art,
So is she mother of man's other part.

She shortly was to drink the dearest blood,
   And yield thy soul away to Satan's cave;
She shortly was thy corse in tomb to shroud,
   And with them all thy diety to have;
Now then in one thou jointly yieldest all,
That several to earth should shortly fall.

O prostrate Christ! erect my crooked mind;
   Lord! let thy fall my flight from earth obtain;
Or if I still must needs in earth be shrined,
   Then, Lord! on earth come fall yet once again;
And either yield with me in earth to lie,
Or else with thee to take me to the sky!

JOSEPH'S AMAZEMENT.

WHEN Christ, by growth, disclosèd His descent
    Into the pure receipt of Mary's breast,
Poor Joseph, stranger yet to God's intent,
    With doubts of jealous thoughts was sore oppress'd;
And, wrought with divers fits of fear and love,
He neither can her free nor faulty prove.

Now sense, the wakeful spy of jealous mind,
    By strong conjectures deemeth her defiled;
But love, in doom of things best lovèd blind,
    Thinks rather sense deceived than her with child;
Yet proofs so pregnant were, that no pretence
Could cloke a thing so clear and plain in sense.

Then Joseph, daunted with a deadly wound,
    Let loose the reigns to undeservèd grief;
His heart did throb, his eyes in tears were drown'd,
    His life a loss, death seem'd his best relief;
The pleasing relish of his former love
In gallish thoughts to taste doth bitter prove.

JOSEPH'S AMAZEMENT.

One foot he often setteth forth of door,
    But t'other's loath uncertain ways to tread ;
He takes his fardel for his needful store,
    He casts his inn where first he means to bed ;
But still ere he can frame his feet to go,
Love winneth time till all conclude in no.

Sometime, grief adding force, he doth depart,
    He will, against his will, keep on his pace ;
But straight remorse so racks his ruing heart,
    That hasting thoughts yield to a pausing space ;
Then mighty reasons press him to remain,
She whom he flies doth win him home again.

But when his thought, by sight of his abode,
    Presents the sign of misesteemèd shame,
Repenting every step that back he trod,
    Tears drown the guides, the tongue the feet doth blame ;
Thus warring with himself a field he fights,
Where every wound upon the giver lights.

And was my love, quoth he, so lightly prized ?
    Or was our sacred league so soon forgot ?
Could vows be void, could virtues be despised ?
    Could such a spouse be stain'd with such a spot ?
O wretched Joseph ! that hast lived so long,
Of faithful love to reap so grievous wrong !

Could such a worm breed in so sweet a wood ?
  Could in so chaste demeanour lurk untruth ?
Could vice lie hid where virtue's image stood ?
  Where hoary sageness gracèd tender youth ?
Where can affiance rest to rest secure ?
In virtue's fairest seat faith is not sure.

All proofs did promise hope a pledge of grace,
  Whose good might have repaid the deepest ill ;
Sweet signs of purest thoughts in saintly face
  Assured the eye of her unstainèd will.
Yet in this seeming lustre seem to lie
Such crimes for which the law condemns to die.

But Joseph's word shall never work her woe :
  I wish her leave to live, not doom to die ;
Though fortune mine, yet am I not her foe,
  She to herself less loving is than I :
The most I will, the less I can, is this,
Sith none may salve, to shun that is amiss.

Exile my home, the wilds shall be my walk,
  Complaints my joy, my music mourning lays ;
With pensive griefs in silence will I talk,
  Sad thoughts shall be my guides in sorrow's
    ways :
This course best suits the care of careless mind,
That seeks to lose what most it joy'd to find.

JOSEPH'S AMAZEMENT.

Like stockèd tree whose branches all do fade,
   Whose leaves do fall and perish'd fruit decay;
Like herb that grows in cold and barren shade,
   Where darkness drives all quick'ning heat away;
So must I die, cut from my root of joy,
And thrown in darkest shades of deep annoy.

But who can fly from that his heart doth feel?
   What change of place can change implanted pain?
Removing moves no hardness from the steel;
   Sick hearts, that shift no fits, shift rooms in vain.
Where thought can see, what helps the closèd eye?
Where heart pursues, what gains the foot to fly?

Yet still I tread a maze of doubtful end;
   I go, I come, she draws, she drives away;
She wounds, she heals, she doth both mar and mend,
   She makes me seek and shun, depart and stay;
She is a friend to love, a foe to loathe,
And in suspense I hang between them both.

NEW PRINCE, NEW POMP.

BEHOLD a silly tender babe,
   In freezing winter night,
In homely manger trembling lies;
   Alas! a piteous sight.

The inns are full, no man will yield
   This little pilgrim bed;
But forced he is with silly beasts
   In crib to shroud his head.

Despise him not for lying there,
   First what he is enquire;
An orient pearl is often found
   In depth of dirty mire.

Weigh not his crib, his wooden dish,
   Nor beast that by him feed;
Weigh not his mother's poor attire,
   Nor Joseph's simple weed.

This stable is a prince's court,
   The crib his chair of state;
The beasts are parcel of his pomp,
   The wooden dish his plate.

The persons in that poor attire
  His royal liveries wear;
The Prince Himself is come from heaven,
  This pomp is praisèd there.

With joy approach, O Christian wight!
  Do homage to thy King;
And highly praise this humble pomp
  Which He from heaven doth bring.

THE BURNING BABE.

AS I in hoary winter's night stood shivering in the snow,
Surprised I was with sudden heat which made my heart to glow;
And lifting up a fearful eye to view what fire was near,
A pretty babe all burning bright did in the air appear,
Who scorchèd with exceeding heat such floods of tears did shed,
As though His floods should quench His flames with what His tears were fed;
Alas! quoth He, but newly born in fiery heats of fry,
Yet none approach to warm their hearts or feel my fire but I!
My faultless breast the furnace is, the fuel wounding thorns;
Love is the fire and sighs the smoke, the ashes shame and scorns;
The fuel Justice layeth on, and Mercy blows the coals;
The metal in this furnace wrought are men's defiled souls;

THE BURNING BABE.

For which, as now on fire I am, to work them to their good,
So will I melt into a bath, to wash them in my blood:
With this He vanish'd out of sight, and swiftly shrunk away,
And straight I callèd unto mind that it was Christmas-day.

NEW HEAVEN, NEW WAR.

COME to your heaven, you heavenly quires!
   Earth hath the heaven of your desires;
   Remove your dwelling to your God,
A stall is now His best abode;
Sith men their homage doth deny,
Come, angels, all their faults supply.

His chilling cold doth heat require,
Come, seraphim, in lieu of fire;
This little ark no cover hath,
Let cherubs' wings his body swathe;
Come, Raphael, this babe must eat,
Provide our little Toby meat.

Let Gabriel be now His groom,
That first took up His earthly room;
Let Michael stand in His defence,
Whom love hath link'd to feeble sense;
Let graces rock when He doth cry,
And angels sing this lullaby.

NEW HEAVEN, NEW WAR.

The same you saw in heavenly seat,
Is He that now sucks Mary's teat;
Agnize your King a mortal wight,
His borrow'd weed lets not your sight;
Come, kiss the manger where He lies;
That is your bliss above the skies.

This little babe so few days old,
Is come to rifle Satan's fold;
All hell doth at His presence quake,
Though He Himself for cold do shake;
For in this weak unarmèd wise
The gates of hell He will surprise.

With tears He fights and wins the field,
His naked breast stands for a shield,
His battering shot are babish cries,
His arrows, looks of weeping eyes,
His martial ensigns, cold and need,
And feeble flesh His warrior's steed.

His camp is pitchèd in a stall,
His bulwark but a broken wall,
His crib His trench, hay-stalks His stakes,
Of shepherds He His muster makes;
And thus, as sure His foe to wound,
The angels' trumps alarum sound.

My soul, with Christ join thou in fight;
Stick to the tents that He hath pight;
Within His crib is surest ward,
This little babe will be thy guard;
If thou wilt foil thy foes with joy,
Then flit not from this heavenly boy.

MÆONIÆ:

OR CERTAIN EXCELLENT POEMS
AND SPIRITUAL HYMNS.
COMPOSED BY
R. S.

LONDON:
PRINTED BY J. HAVILAND.
1634.

THE VIRGIN MARY'S CONCEPTION.

UR second Eve puts on her mortal shroud,
    Earth breeds a heaven for God's new
        dwelling-place;
Now riseth up Elias' little cloud,
    That growing shall distil the showers of grace;
Her being now begins, who, ere she ends,
Shall bring our good that shall our evil mend.

Both grace and nature did their force unite
    To make this babe the sum of all their best;
Our most her least, our million but her mite,
    She was at easiest rate worth all the rest:
What grace to men or angels God did part,
Was all united in this infant's heart.

Four only wights bred without fault are named,
    And all the rest conceivèd were in sin;
Without both man and wife was Adam framed,
    Of man, but not of wife, did Eve begin;
Wife without touch of man Christ's mother was,
Of man and wife this babe was bred in grace.

HER NATIVITY.

JOY in the rising of our orient star
   That shall bring forth the sun that lent her
      light;
Joy in the peace that shall conclude our war,
   And soon rebate the edge of Satan's spite;
Loadstar of all engulf'd in worldly waves,
The card and compass that from shipwreck saves.

The patriarchs and prophets were the flowers
   Which time by course of ages did distil,
And call'd into this little cloud the showers
   Whose gracious drops the world with joy shall
      fill;
Whose moisture suppli'th every soul with grace,
And bringeth life to Adam's dying race.

For God in earth she is the royal throne,
   The chosen cloth to make His mortal weed;
The quarry to cut out our corner-stone,
   Soil full of, yet free from, all mortal seed;
For heavenly flower she is the Jesse rod,
The child of man, the parent of a God.

HER ESPOUSALS.

WIFE did she live, yet virgin did she die,
    Untouch'd of man, yet mother of a son;
    To save herself and child from fatal lie,
To end the web whereof the thread was spun,
In marriage knots to Joseph she was tied,
Unwonted works with wonted veils to hide.

God lent His paradise to Joseph's care,
    Wherein he was to plant the tree of life;
This Son of Joseph's child the title bare,
    Just cause to make the mother Joseph's wife.
Oh! blessèd man, betroth'd to such a spouse,
More bless'd to live with such a child in house!

No carnal love this sacred league procured,
    All vain delights were far from their assent;
Though both in wedlock bands themselves assured,
    Yet chaste by vow they seal'd their chaste intent:
Thus had she virgins', wives', and widows' crown,
And by chaste childbirth doubled her renown.

THE VIRGIN'S SALUTATION.

SPELL Eva back and Ave shall you find,
    The first began, the last reversed our
        harms:
An angel's witching words did Eva blind,
    An angel's Ave disenchants the charms:
Death first by woman's weakness enter'd in,
In woman's virtue life doth now begin.

O virgin breast! the heavens to thee incline,
    In thee their joy and sovereign they agnize;
Too mean their glory is to match with thine,
    Whose chaste receipt God more than heaven
        did prize.
Hail! fairest heaven, that heaven and earth did
    bless,
Where virtue's star God's sun of justice is!

With haughty mind to Godhead man aspired,
    And was by pride from place of pleasure chased;
With loving mind our manhood God desired,
    And as by love in greater pleasure placed;
Man labouring to ascend procured our fall,
God yielding to descend cut off our thrall.

THE VISITATION.

PROCLAIMED queen and mother of a God,
   The light of earth, the sovereign of saints,
With pilgrim foot up tiring hills she trod,
And heavenly style with handmaids' toil ac-
  quaints:
Her youth to age, herself to sick she lends,
Her heart to God, to neighbour hand she bends.

A prince she is, and mightier prince doth bear,
   Yet pomp of princely train she would not have;
But doubtless heavenly quires attendant were,
   Her child from harm, herself from fall to save:
Word to the voice, song to the tune she brings,
The voice her word, the tune her ditty sings.

Eternal lights enclosèd in her breast
   Shot out such piercing beams of burning love,
That when her voice her cousin's ears possess'd,
   The force thereof did force her babe to move:
With secret signs the children greet each other,
But open praise each leaveth to his mother.

THE NATIVITY OF CHRIST.*

BEHOLD the father is his daughter's son,
    The bird that built the nest is hatch'd
        therein,
The old of years an hour hath not outrun,
    Eternal life to live doth now begin,
The word is dumb, the mirth of heaven doth weep,
Might feeble is, and force doth faintly creep.

O dying souls! behold your living spring!
    O dazzled eyes! behold your son of grace!
Dull ears attend what word this word doth bring!
    Up, heavy hearts, with joy your joy embrace!
From death, from dark, from deafness, from
    despairs,
This life, this light, this word, this joy repairs.

Gift better than Himself God doth not know,
    Gift better than his God no man can see;
This gift doth here the giver given bestow,
    Gift to this gift let each receiver be:
God is my gift, Himself he freely gave me,
God's gift am I, and none but God shall have me.

* Transferred from the Edition of "St. Peter's Complaint" of 1634.

THE NATIVITY OF CHRIST.

Man alter'd was by sin from man to beast ;
    Beast's food is hay, hay is all mortal flesh ;
Now God is flesh, and lives in manger press'd,
    As hay the brutest sinner to refresh :
Oh happy field wherein this fodder grew,
Whose taste doth us from beasts to men renew !

HIS CIRCUMCISION.

THE head is lanced to work the body's cure,
    With ang'ring salve it smarts to heal our
        wound;
To faultless Son, from all offences pure,
    The faulty vassel's scourges do redound;
The judge is cast, the guilty to acquit,
The sun defaced, to lend the star his light..

The vein of life distilleth drops of grace,
    Our rock gives issue to a heavenly spring;
Tears from his eyes, blood streams from wounded
        place,
    With showers to heaven of joy a harvest bring:
This sacred dew let angels gather up,
Such dainty drops best fit their nectar'd cup.

With weeping eyes His mother rued His smart,
    If blood from him, tears came from her as fast;
The knife that cut His flesh did pierce her heart,
    The pain that Jesu felt did Mary taste:
His life and her's hung by one fatal twist,
No blow that hit the Son the mother miss'd.

THE EPIPHANY.

To blaze the rising of this glorious sun
    A glittering star appeareth in the east,
  Whose sight to pilgrim toils three sages won
  To seek the light they long had in request;
And by this star to nobler star they pass,
Whose arms did their desirèd sun embrace.

Still was the sky wherein these planets shined,
    And want the cloud that did eclipse their rays;
Yet through this cloud their light did passage find,
    And pierced these sages' hearts by secret ways,
Which made them know the Ruler of the skies,
By infant's tongue and looks of babish eyes.

Heaven at her light, earth blusheth at her pride,
    And of their pomp these peers ashamèd be;
Their crowns, their robes, their trains they set
    aside,
    When God's poor cottage clouts and crew they
    see;
All glorious things their glory now despise,
Sith God contempt doth more than glory prize.

Three gifts they brought, three gifts they bear
    away;
  For incense, mirth and gold, faith, hope and
    love;
And with their gifts the givers' hearts do stay,
  Their mind from Christ no parting can remove;
His humble state, his stall, his poor retinue,
They fancy more than all their rich revenue.

THE PRESENTATION.

To be redeem'd the world's Redeemer brought,
    Two silly turtle-doves for ransom pays;
  Oh! ware with empires worthy to be bought,
This easy rate doth sound, not drown thy praise!
For sith no price can to thy worth amount,
A dove, yea love, due price thou dost account.

Old Simeon cheap pennyworth and sweet
    Obtain'd, when Thee in arms he did embrace;
His weeping eyes Thy smiling looks did meet,
    Thy love his heart, Thy kisses bless'd his face;
O eyes! O heart! mean sights and loves avoid,
Base not yourselves, your best you have enjoy'd!

O virgin pure! thou dost these doves present
    As due to law, not as an equal price;
To buy such ware thou wouldst thyself have spent;
    The world to reach His worth could not suffice;
If God were to be bought, not worldly pelf,
But thou wert fittest price next God Himself.

THE FLIGHT INTO EGYPT.

ALAS! our Day is forced to fly by night!
    Light without light, and sun by silent shade.
O nature, blush! that sufferest such a wight,
  That in thy sun this dark eclipse hath made;
Day to his eyes, light to his steps deny,
That hates the light which graceth every eye.

Sun being fled the stars do less their light,
    And shining beams in bloody streams they drench;
A cruel storm of Herod's mortal spite
    Their lives and lights with bloody showers doth quench:
The tyrant to be sure of murdering one,
For fear of sparing Him doth pardon none.

O blessed babes! first flowers of Christian spring,
  Who though untimely cropp'd fair garlands frame,
With open throats and silent mouths you sing
  His praise whom age permits you not to name;
Your tunes are tears, your instruments are swords,
Your ditty death, and blood in lieu of words!

CHRIST'S RETURN OUT OF EGYPT.

WHEN Death and Hell their right in Herod
    claim,
  Christ from exile returns to native soil;
There with His life more deeply Death to maim;
  Than Death did life by all the infants spoil.
He show'd the parents, that their babes did moan,
That all their lives were less than His alone.

But hearing Herod's son to have the crown;
  An impious offspring of a bloody sire;
To Nazareth, of heaven beloved town,
  Flower to a flower He fitly doth retire;
For flower He is and in a flower He bred,
And from a throne now to a flower He fled.

And well deserved this flower His fruit to view,
  Where He invested was in mortal weed;
Where first unto a tender bud He grew,
  In virgin branch unstain'd with mortal seed:
Young flower, with flowers in flower well may He be,
Ripe fruit, He must with thorns hang on a tree.

CHRIST'S CHILDHOOD.*

TILL twelve years' age, how Christ His childhood spent
    All earthly pens unworthy were to write;
Such acts to mortal eyes He did present,
    Whose worth not men but angels must recite:
No nature's blots, no childish faults defiled,
Where grace was guide, and God did play the child.

In springing locks lay crouchèd hoary wit,
    In semblant young, a grave and ancient port;
In lowly looks high majesty did sit,
    In tender tongue sound sense of sagest sort:
Nature imparted all that she could teach,
And God supplied where nature could not reach.

His mirth of modest mien a mirror was;
    His sadness temper'd with a mild aspect;
His eye to try each action was a glass,
    Whose looks did good approve and bad correct;
His nature's gifts, His grace, His word and deed,
Well showed that all did from a God proceed.

* Transferred from the Edition of "St. Peter's Complaint" of 1634.

CHRIST'S BLOODY SWEAT.

FAT soil, full spring, sweet olive, grape of
  bliss,
 That yields, that streams, that pours, that
  doth distil,
Untill'd, undrawn, unstamp'd, untouch'd of press,
 Dear fruit, clear brooks, fair oil, sweet wine at
  will,
Thus Christ unforced prevents, in shedding blood,
The whips, the thorns, the nails, the spear and rood.

He pelican's, he phœnix' fate doth prove,
 Whom flames consume, whom streams enforce
  to die;
How burneth blood, how bleedeth burning love?
 Can one in flame and stream both bathe and fry?
How could He join a phœnix' fiery pains
In fainting pelican's still bleeding veins?

Elias once, to prove God's sovereign power,
 By prayer procured a fire of wond'rous force,
That blood and water and wood did devour,
 Yea stones and dust beyond all nature's course:
Such fire is love that, fed with gory blood,
Doth burn no less than in the driest wood.

O sacred fire! come show thy force on me,
    That sacrifice to Christ I may return:
If wither'd wood for fuel fittest be,
    If stones and dust, if flesh and blood will burn,
I wither'd am and stony to all good,
A sack of dust, a mass of flesh and blood.

CHRIST'S SLEEPING FRIENDS.

WHEN Christ with care and pangs of death
    oppress'd,
    From frighted flesh a bloody sweat did
rain ;
And, full of fear, without repose or rest,
    In agony did pray and watch in pain ;
Three sundry times He His disciples finds
With heavy eyes, but far more heavy minds.

With mild rebuke He warnèd them to wake,
    Yet sleep did still their drowsy senses hold ;
As, when the sun the brightest shew doth make,
    In darkness shrouds the night-birds them enfold ;
His foes did watch to work their cruel spite,
His drowsy friends slept in His hardest plight.

As Jonas sailèd once from Joppa's shore
    A boisterous tempest in the air did broil,
The waves did rage, the thundering heavens did
    roar,
    The storms, the rocks, the lightnings threaten'd
    spoil ;
The ship was billows' game and chance's prey,
Yet careless Jonas mute and sleeping lay.

CHRIST'S SLEEPING FRIENDS.

So now, though Judas, like a blust'ring gust,
   Do stir the furious sea of Jewish ire,
Though storming troops, in quarrels most unjust,
   Against the back of all our bliss conspire,
Yet these disciples sleeping lie secure,
As though their wonted calm did still endure.

So Jonas once, his weary limbs to rest,
   Did shroud himself in pleasant ivy shade,
But lo! while him a heavy sleep opprest,
   His shadowy bower to wither'd stalks did fade;
A canker-worm had gnawn the root away,
And brought the glorious branches to decay.

O gracious plant! O tree of heavenly spring!
   The paragon for leaf, for fruit and flower,
How sweet a shadow did Thy branches bring
   To shroud these souls that chose Thee for their bower!
But now while they with Jonas fall asleep,
To spoil their plant an envious worm doth creep.

Awake, ye slumbering wights! lift up your eyes,
   Mark Judas, how to tear your root he strives;
Alas! the glory of your arbour dies,
   Arise and guard the comfort of your lives;
No Jonas' ivy, no Zaccheus' tree,
Were to the world so great a loss as He.

THE VIRGIN MARY TO CHRIST ON THE CROSS.

WHAT mist hath dimm'd that glorious
    face?
What seas of grief my sun doth toss?
The golden rays of heavenly grace
    Lie now eclipsèd on the cross.

Jesus, my love, my Son, my God,
    Behold Thy mother wash'd in tears:
Thy bloody wounds be made a rod
    To chasten these my later years.

You cruel Jews, come work your ire
    Upon this worthless flesh of mine,
And kindle not eternal fire
    By wounding Him who is divine.

Thou messenger that didst impart
    His first descent into my womb,
Come help me now to cleave my heart,
    That there I may my Son entomb.

MARY TO CHRIST ON THE CROSS.

You angels, all that present were
    To show His birth with harmony,
Why are you not now ready here,
    To make a mourning symphony?

The cause I know you wail alone,
    And shed your tears in secrecy,
Lest I should movèd be to moan,
    By force of heavy company.

But wail, my soul, thy comfort dies,
    My woeful womb, lament thy fruit;
My heart give tears unto mine eyes,
    Let sorrow string my heavy lute.

A HOLY HYMN.*

PRAISE, O Sion! praise thy Saviour,
  Praise thy captain and thy pastor,
    With hymns and solemn harmony.
What power affords perform in deed;
His worths all praises far exceed,
    No praise can reach his dignity.

A special theme of praise is read,
A living and life-giving bread,
    Is on this day exhibited;
Which in the supper of our Lord,
To twelve disciples at His board
    None doubts was delivered.

Let our praise be loud and free,
Full of joy and decent glee,
    With minds' and voices' melody;
For now solemnize we that day,
Which doth with joy to us display
    The prince of this mystery.

* Version of the "Lauda Syon Salvatorem" of St. Thomas Aquinas.

At this board of our new ruler,
Of new law, new paschal order
   The ancient rite abolisheth;
Old decrees be new annullèd,
Shadows are in truths fulfillèd,
   Day former darkness finisheth.

That at supper Christ performèd,
To be done He straitly charged
   For His eternal memory.
Guided by His sacred orders,
Bread and wine upon our altars
   To saving host we sanctify.

Christians are by faith assurèd
That to flesh the bread is changèd,
   The wine to blood most precious:
That no wit nor sense conceiveth,
Firm and grounded faith believeth,
   In strange effects not curious.*

---

* The following twenty-four lines are omitted in the edition of 1630, and in their place are substituted,—

> "As staff of bread thy heart sustains,
> And cheerful wine thy strength regains,
>   By power and virtue natural;
> So doth this consecrated food,
> The symbol of Christ's flesh and blood,
>   By virtue supernatural.
>
> The ruins of thy soul repair,
> Banish sin, horror and despair,
>   And feed faith, by faith received:
> Angel's bread," &c.

A HOLY HYMN.

Under kinds two in appearance,
Two in show but one in substance,
   Lie things beyond comparison;
Flesh is meat, blood drink most heavenly,
Yet is Christ in each kind wholly,
   Most free from all division.

None that eateth Him doth chew Him,
None that takes Him doth divide Him,
   Received He whole persevereth.
Be there one or thousands hosted,
One as much as all receivèd,
   He by no eating perisheth.

Both the good and bad receive Him,
But effects are diverse in them,
   True life or due destruction.
Life to the good, death to the wicked,
Mark how both alike receivèd
   With far unlike conclusion.

When the priest the host divideth,
Know that in each part abideth
   All that the whole host covered.
Form of bread, not Christ is broken,
Not of Christ, but of His token,
   Is state or stature altered.

A HOLY HYMN.

Angels' bread made pilgrim's feeding,
Truly bread for children's eating,
   To dogs not to be offerèd.
Signed by Isaac on the altar,
By the lamb and paschal supper,
   And in the manna figurèd.

Jesu, food and feeder of us,
Here with mercy feed and friend us,
   Then grant in heaven felicity!
Lord of all, whom here Thou feedest,
Fellows, heirs, guests with Thy dearest,
   Make us in heavenly company! Amen.

SAINT PETER'S AFFLICTED MIND.

IF that the sick may groan,
   Or orphan mourn his loss :
If wounded wretch may rue his harms,
   Or caitiff show his cross ;

If heart consumed with care,
   May utter signs of pain ;
Then may my breast be sorrow's home,
   And tongue with cause complain.

My malady is sin,
   And languor of the mind ;
My body but a Lazar's couch
   Wherein my soul is pined.

The care of heavenly kind
   Is dead to my relief ;
Forlorn, and left like orphan child,
   With sighs I feed my grief.

My wounds, with mortal smart
   My dying soul torment,
And, prisoner to my own mishaps,
   My folly I repent.

130 ST. PETER'S AFFLICTED MIND.

    My heart is but the haunt
        Where all dislike doth keep;
    And who can blame so lost a wretch,
        Though tears of blood he weep?

SAINT PETER'S REMORSE.

REMORSE upbraids my faults;
    Self-blaming conscience cries;
Sin claims the host of humbled thoughts
    And streams of weeping eyes:

Let penance, Lord, prevail;
    Let sorrow sue release;
Let love be umpire in my cause,
    And pass the doom of peace.

If doom go by desert,
    My least desert is death;
That robs from soul's immortal joys,
    From body mortal breath.

But in so high a God,
    So base a worm's annoy
Can add no praise unto Thy power,
    No bliss unto Thy joy.

Well may I fry in flames,
    Due fuel to hell-fire!
But on a wretch to wreak Thy wrath
    Cannot be worth Thine ire.

ST. PETER'S REMORSE.

Yet sith so vile a worm
    Hath wrought his greatest spite,
Of highest treasons well Thou may'st
    In rigour him indite.

But Mercy may relent,
    And temper Justice' rod,
For mercy doth as much belong
    As justice to a God.

If former time or place
    More right to mercy win,
Thou first were author of myself,
    Then umpire of my sin.

Did Mercy spin the thread
    To weave in Justice' loom,
Wert then a father to conclude
    With dreadful judge's doom.

It is a small relief
    To say I was Thy child,
If, as an ill-deserving foe,
    From grace I am exiled.

I was, I had, I could,
    All words importing want;
They are but dust of dead supplies,
    Where needful helps are scant.

ST. PETER'S REMORSE.

Once to have been in bliss
   That hardly can return,
Doth but bewray from whence I fell,
   As wherefore now I mourn.

All thoughts of passèd hopes
   Increase my present cross;
Like ruins of decayèd joys,
   They still upbraid my loss.

O mild and mighty Lord!
   Amend that is amiss;
My sin my sore, Thy love my salve,
   Thy cure my comfort is.

Confirm thy former deed,
   Reform that is defiled;
I was, I am, I will remain
   Thy charge, Thy choice, Thy child.

MAN TO THE WOUND IN CHRIST'S SIDE.

PLEASANT spot! O place of rest!
   O royal rift! O worthy wound!
Come harbour me, a weary guest,
   That in the world no ease have found!

I lie lamenting at Thy gate,
   Yet dare I not adventure in:
I bear with me a troublous mate,
   And cumber'd am with heaps of sin.

Discharge me of this heavy load,
   That easier passage I may find,
Within this bower to make abode,
   And in this glorious tomb be shrined.

Here must I live, here must I die,
   Here would I utter all my grief;
Here would I all those pains descry,
   Which here did meet for my relief.

Here would I view that bloody sore,
   Which dint of spiteful spear did breed :

The bloody wounds laid there in store,
  Would force a stony heart to bleed.

Here is the spring of trickling tears,
  The mirror of all mourning wights,
With doleful tunes for dumpish ears,
  And solemn shows for sorrow'd sights.

Oh, happy soul, that flies so high
  As to attain this sacred cave!
Lord, send me wings, that I may fly,
  And in this harbour quiet have!

UPON THE IMAGE OF DEATH.

BEFORE my face the picture hangs,
    That daily should put me in mind.
Of those cold names and bitter pangs,
    That shortly I am like to find:
But yet, alas! full little I
Do think hereon that I must die.

I often look upon a face
    Most ugly, grisly, bare and thin;
I often view the hollow place,
    Where eyes and nose had sometime been:
I see the bones across that lie,
Yet little think that I must die.

I read the label underneath,
    That telleth me whereto I must;
I see the sentence eke that saith,
    Remember, man, thou art but dust:
But yet, alas! but seldom I
Do think indeed that I must die.

Continually at my bed's head
    An hearse doth hang, which doth me tell

UPON THE IMAGE OF DEATH.

That I ere morning may be dead,
   Though now I feel myself full well :
But yet, alas! for all this I
Have little mind that I must die.

The gown which I do use to wear,
   The knife wherewith I cut my meat,
And eke that old and ancient chair
   Which is my only usual seat :
All these do tell me I must die,
And yet my life amend not I.

My ancestors are turned to clay,
   And many of my mates are gone;
My youngers daily drop away,
   And can I think to 'scape alone ?
No, no, I know that I must die,
And yet my life amend not I.

Not Solomon, for all his wit,
   Nor Samson, though he were so strong,
No king nor person ever yet
   Could 'scape, but Death laid him along :
Wherefore I know that I must die,
   And yet my life amend not I.

Though all the East did quake to hear
   Of Alexander's dreadful name,
And all the West did likewise fear
   To hear of Julius Cæsar's fame,

UPON THE IMAGE OF DEATH.

Yet both by Death in dust now lie;
Who can then 'scape, but he must die?

If none can 'scape Death's dreadful dart,
   If rich and poor his beck obey;
If strong, if wise, if all do smart,
   Then I to 'scape shall have no way.
Oh! grant me grace, O God! that I
My life may mend, sith I must die.

A VALE OF TEARS.

A VALE there is, enwrapt with dreadful
 shades,
 Which thick of mourning pines shrouds
from the sun,
Where hanging cliffs yield short and dumpish
 glades,
 And snowy flood with broken streams doth run.

Where eye-room is from rock to cloudy sky,
 From thence to dales with stony ruins strew'd,
Then to the crushèd water's frothy fry,
 Which tumbleth from the tops where snow is
 thaw'd.

Where ears of other sound can have no choice,
 But various blust'ring of the stubborn wind
In trees, in caves, in straits with divers noise;
 Which now doth hiss, now howl, now roar by
 kind.

Where waters wrestle with encount'ring stones,
 That break their streams and turn them into
 foam,

A VALE OF TEARS.

The hollow clouds full fraught with thund'ring
    groans,
  With hideous thumps discharge their pregnant
    womb.

And in the horror of this fearful quire
  Consists the music of this doleful place;
All pleasant birds from thence their tunes retire,
  Where none but heavy notes have any grace.

Resort there is of none but pilgrim wights,
  That pass with trembling foot and panting heart,
With terror cast in cold and shivering frights,
  They judge the place to terror framed by art.

Yet nature's work it is, of art untouch'd,
  So strait indeed, so vast unto the eye,
With such disorder'd order strangely couch'd,
  And with such pleasing horror low and high,

That who it views must needs remain aghast,
  Much at the work, more at the Maker's might;
And muse how nature such a plot could cast
  Where nothing seemeth wrong, yet nothing right.

A place for mated minds, an only bower
  Where everything do soothe a dumpish mood;
Earth lies forlorn; the cloudy sky doth lower,
  The wind here weeps, here sighs, here cries aloud.

A VALE OF TEARS.

The struggling flood between the marble groans,
    Then roaring beats upon the craggy sides;
A little off, amidst the pebble stones,
    With bubbling streams and purling noise it glides.

The pines thick set, high grown and ever green,
    Still clothe the place with sad and mourning veil;
Here gaping cliff, there mossy plain is seen,
    Here hope doth spring, and there again doth quail.

Huge massy stones that hang by tickle stays,
    Still threaten fall, and seem to hang in fear;
Some wither'd trees, ashamed of their decays,
    Bereft of green are forced grey coats to wear.

Here crystal springs crept out of secret vein,
    Straight find some envious hole that hides their grace;
Here searèd tufts lament the want of rain,
    There thunder-wrack gives terror to the place.

All pangs and heavy passions here may find
    A thousand motives suiting to their griefs,
To feed the sorrows of their troubled mind,
    And chase away dame Pleasure's vain reliefs.

To plaining thoughts this vale a rest may be,
    To which from worldly joys they may retire;
Where sorrow springs from water, stone and tree;
    Where everything with mourners doth conspire.

A VALE OF TEARS.

Set here, my soul, main streams of tears afloat,
   Here all thy sinful foils alone recount;
Of solemn tunes make thou the doleful note,
   That, by thy ditties, dolour may amount.

When echoes shall repeat thy painful cries,
   Think that the very stones thy sins bewray,
And now accuse thee with their sad replies,
   As heaven and earth shall in the latter day.

Let former faults be fuel of thy fire,
   For grief in limbeck of thy heart to still
Thy pensive thoughts and dumps of thy desire,
   And vapour tears up to thy eyes at will.

Let tears to tunes, and pains to plaints be press'd,
   And let this be the burden of thy song,—
Come, deep remorse, possess my sinful breast;
   Delights, adieu! I harbour'd you too long.

THE PRODIGAL CHILD'S SOUL WRACK.

DISANCHOR'D from a blissful shore,
    And launch'd into the main of cares;
Grown rich in vice, in virtue poor,
From freedom fall'n in fatal snares;

I found myself on every side
    Enwrappèd in the waves of woe,
And, tossèd with a toilsome tide,
    Could to no port for refuge go.

The wrestling winds with raging blasts,
    Still held me in a cruel chase;
They broke my anchors, sails and masts,
    Permitting no reposing place.

The boisterous seas, with swelling floods,
    On every side did work their spite,
Heaven, overcast with stormy clouds,
    Denied the planets' guiding light.

The hellish furies lay in wait
    To win my soul into their power,
To make me bite at every bait,
    Wherein my bane I might devour.

Thus heaven and earth, thus sea and land,
    Thus storms and tempests did conspire,
With just revenge of scourging hand,
    To witness God's deservèd ire.

I plungèd in this heavy plight,
    Found in my faults just cause of fear;
By darkness taught to know my light,
    The loss thereof enforcèd tears.

I felt my inward bleeding sores,
    My fester'd wounds began to smart,
Stept far within death's fatal doors,
    The pangs thereof were near my heart.

I cried a truce, I craved a peace,
    A league with death I would conclude;
But vain it was to sue release,
    Subdue I must or be subdued.

Death and deceit had pitch'd their snares,
    And put their wicked proofs in ure,
To sink me in despairing cares,
    Or make me stoop to pleasure's lure.

They sought by their bewitching charms
    So to enchant my erring sense,
That when they sought my greatest harms,
    I might neglect my best defence.

SOUL WRACK.

My dazzled eyes could take no view,
  No heed of their deceiving shifts,
So often did they alter hue,
  And practise new devisèd drifts.

With Syren's song they fed my ears,
  Till, lull'd asleep in Error's lap,
I found these tunes turn'd into tears,
  And short delights to long mishap.

For I enticèd to their lore,
  And soothèd with their idle toys,
Was trainèd to their prison door,—
  The end of all such flying joys.

Where chain'd in sin I lay in thrall,
  Next to the dungeon of despair,
Till Mercy raised me from my fall,
  And Grace my ruins did repair.

MAN'S CIVIL WAR.

MY hovering thoughts would fly to heaven,
    And quiet nestle in the sky;
Fain would my ship in virtue's shore
    Without remove at anchor lie;

But mounting thoughts are haled down
    With heavy poise of mortal load;
And blustering storms deny my ship
    In virtue's haven secure abode.

When inward eye to heavenly sights
    Doth draw my longing heart's desire,
The world with jesses of delights
    Would to her perch my thoughts retire.

Fond Fancy trains to Pleasure's lure,
    Though Reason stiffly do repine;
Though Wisdom woo me to the saint,
    Yet Sense would win me to the shrine.

Where wisdom loathes, there fancy loves,
    And overrules the captive will;
Foes senses are to virtue's lore,
    They draw the wit their wish to fill.

Need craves consent of soul to sense,
  Yet divers bents breed civil fray;
Hard hap where halves must disagree,
  Or truce of halves the whole betray!

O cruel fight! where fighting friend
  With love doth kill a favouring foe;
Where peace with sense is war with God,
  And self-delight the seed of woe!

Dame Pleasure's drugs are steep'd in sin,
  Their sugar'd taste doth breed annoy;
O fickle Sense! beware her gin,
  Sell not thy soul for brittle joy!

SEEK FLOWERS OF HEAVEN.

SOAR up, my soul, unto thy rest,
    Cast off this loathsome load;
Long is the death of thine exile,
    Too long thy strict abode.

Graze not on worldly wither'd wood,
    It fitteth not thy taste;
The flowers of everlasting spring
    Do grow for thy repast.

Their leaves are stain'd in beauty's dye,
    And blazèd with her beams,
Their stalks enamel'd with delight,
    And limn'd with glorious gleams.

Life-giving juice of living love
    Their sugar'd veins doth fill,
And water'd with eternal showers
    They nectar'd drops distill.

These flowers do spring from fertile soil,
    Though from unmanured field;
Most glittering gold in lieu of glebe,
    These fragrant flowers do yield.

SEEK FLOWERS OF HEAVEN. ·149

Whose sovereign scent surpassing sense
    So ravisheth the mind,
That worldly weeds needs must he loathe
    That can these flowers find.

ADDITIONAL POEMS.

DECEASE, RELEASE, DUM MORIOR, ORIOR.*

[Addl. MSS. Brit. Mus. No. 10,422.]

THE pounded spice both taste and scent doth please,
   In fading smoke the force doth incense show;
The perish'd kernel springeth with increase,
   The loppèd tree doth best and soonest grow.

God's spice I was, and pounding was my due,
   In fading breath my incense favour'd best;
Death was my mean my kernel to renew,
   By lopping shot I up to heavenly rest.

Some things more perfect are in their decay,
   Like spark that going out gives clearest light;
Such was my hap whose doleful dying day
   Began my joy, and termèd Fortune's spite.

* On the Death of the martyred Mary Stuart, Queen of Scots.

DECEASE, RELEASE.

Alive a Queen, now dead I am a Saint ;
    Once Mary call'd, my name now Martyr is ;
From earthly reign debarrèd by restraint,
    In lieu whereof I reign in heavenly bliss.

My life my grief, my death hath wrought my joy,
    My friends my foil, my foes my weal procured ;
My speedy death hath scornèd long annoy,
    And loss of life and endless life assured.

My scaffold was the bed where ease I found,
    The block a pillow of eternal rest ;
My headman cast me in a blissful swound,
    His axe cut off my cares from cumber'd breast.

Rue not my death, rejoice at my repose ;
    It was no death to me, but to my woe ;
The bud was open'd to let out the rose,
    The chains unloosed to let the captive go.

A prince by birth, a prisoner by mishap,
    From crown to cross, from throne to thrall I fell;
My right my ruth, my titles wrought my trap,
    My weal my woe, my worldly heaven my hell.

By death from prisoner to a prince enhanced,
    From cross to crown, from thrall to throne again ;
My ruth my right, my trap my style advanced
    From woe to weal, from hell to heavenly reign.

I DIE WITHOUT DESERT.*

[Addl. MSS. Brit. Mus. No. 10,422.]

If orphan child, enwrapt in swathing bands,
   Doth move to mercy when forlorn it lies;
If none without remorse of love withstands
   The piteous noise of infant's silly cries;
Then hope, my helpless heart, some tender cares
Will rue thy orphan state and feeble tears.

Relinquish'd lamb, in solitary wood,
   With dying bleat doth move the toughest mind;
The gasping pangs of new engender'd brood,
   Base though they be, compassion use to find:
Why should I then of pity doubt to speed,
Whose hap would force the hardest heart to bleed?

Left orphan-like in helpless state I rue,
   With only sighs and tears I plead my case;
My dying plaints I daily do renew,
   And fill with heavy noise a desert place:
Some tender heart will weep to hear my moan
Men pity may, but help me God alone!

* Presumed to be on the same subject.

I DIE WITHOUT DESERT.

Rain down, ye heavens, your tears this case requires;
   Man's eyes unable are enough to shed;
If sorrows could have place in heavenly quires,
   A juster ground the world hath seldom bred:
For right is wrong, and virtue waged with blood;
The bad are bless'd, God murder'd in the good.

A gracious plant for fruit, for leaf and flower,
   A peerless gem for virtue, proof, and price,
A noble peer for prowess, will, and power,
   A friend to truth, a foe I was to vice;
And lo! alas! now innocent I die,
A case that might make even the stones to cry.

Thus fortune's favours still are bent to flight,
   Thus worldly bliss in final bale doth end;
Thus virtue still pursuèd is with spite,
   But let my fate though rueful none offend:
God doth sometimes crop first the sweetest flower,
And leave the weed till time do it devour.

OF THE BLESSED SACRAMENT OF THE ALTAR.

[Addl. MSS. Brit. Mus. No. 10,422.]

IN paschal feast, the end of ancient rite,
    An entrance to never-ending grace,
    Types to the truth, dim gleams to the light,
Performing deed presaging signs did chase:
Christ's final meal was fountain of our good,
For mortal meat He gave immortal food.

That which He gave He was, oh, peerless gift!
    Both God and man He was, and both He gave.
He in His hands Himself did truly lift,
    Far off they see whom in themselves they have;
Twelve did He feed, twelve did their feeder eat,
He made, He dress'd, He gave, He was their meat.

They saw, they heard, they felt Him sitting near,
    Unseen, unfelt, unheard, they Him received;
No diverse thing, though diverse it appear,
    Though senses fail, yet faith is not deceived;
And if the wonder of their work be new,
Believe the worker 'cause His word is true.

Here truth belief, belief inviteth love,
  So sweet a truth love never yet enjoy'd ;
What thought can think, what will doth best
    approve,
  Is here obtain'd where no desire is void :
The grace, the joy, the treasure here is such,
No wit can wish, nor will embrace so much.

Self-love here cannot crave more than it finds ;
  Ambition to no higher worth aspire ;
The eagerest famine of most hungry minds
  May fill, yea far exceed, their own desire :
In sum here is all in a sum express'd,
Of which the most of every good the best.

To ravish eyes here heavenly beauties are ;
  To win the ear sweet music's sweetest sound ;
To lure the taste the angels' heavenly fare ;
  To soothe the scent divine perfumes abound ;
To please the touch He in our hearts doth bed,
Whose touch doth cure the deaf, the dumb, the
    dead.

Here to delight the will true wisdom is ;
  To woo the will of every good the choice ;
For memory a mirror showing bliss,
  Here all that can both sense and soul rejoice ;
And if to all, all this it doth not bring,
The fault is in the men, not in the thing.

Though blind men see no light, the sun doth shine;
   Sweet cates are sweet, though fever'd tastes
     deny it;
Pearls precious are, though trodden on by swine;
   Each truth is true, though all men do not try it;
The best still to the bad doth work the worst;
Things bred to bliss do make the more accursed.

The angels' eyes, whom veils cannot deceive,
   Might best disclose that best they did discern;
Men must with sound and silent faith receive
   More than they can by sense or reason learn;
God's power our proofs, His works our wit exceed,
The doer's might is reason of His deed.

A body is endow'd with ghostly rights;
   A nature's work from nature's law is free;
In heavenly sun lie hid eternal lights,
   Lights clear and near, yet them no eye can see:
Dead forms a never-dying life do shroud:
A boundless sea lies in a little cloud.

The God of hosts in slender host doth dwell,
   Yea, God and man with all to either due;
That God that rules the heavens and rifled hell,
   That man whose death did us to life renew;
That God and man that is the angels' bliss,
In form of bread and wine our nature is.

OF THE BLESSED SACRAMENT.

Whole may His body be in smallest bread,
    Whole in the whole, yea whole in every crumb ;
With which be one or [even] ten thousand fed,
    All to each one, to all but one doth come ;
And though each one as much as all receive,
Not one too much, nor all too little have.

One soul in man is all in every part ;
    One face at once in many mirrors shines ;
One fearful noise doth make a thousand start ;
    One eye at once of countless things defines ;
If proofs of one in many Nature frame,
God may in stronger sort perform the same.

God present is at once in every place,
    Yet God in every place is ever one ;
So may there be by gifts of ghostly grace,
    One man in many rooms, yet filling none ;
Sith angels may effects of bodies show,
God angels' gifts on bodies may bestow.

What God as author made He alter may ;
    No change so hard as making all of nought ;
If Adam framèd were of slimy clay,
    Bread may to Christ's most sacred flesh be wrought :
He may do this that made with mighty hand
Of water wine, a snake of Moses's wand.

THE DEATH OF OUR LADY.

[Addl. MSS. Brit. Mus. No. 10,422.]

WEEP, living things, of life the mother dies;
    The world doth lose the sum of all her bliss,
The queen of earth, the empress of the skies;
    By Mary's death mankind an orphan is:
Let nature weep, yea let all graces moan,
Their glory, grace, and gifts die all in one.

It was no death to her, but to her woe,
    By which her joys began, her griefs did end;
Death was to her a friend, to us a foe,
    Life of whose lives did on her life depend:
Not prey of death, but praise to death she was,
Whose ugly shape seem'd glorious in her face.

Her face a heaven, two planets were her eyes,
    Whose gracious light did make our clearest day;
But one such heaven there was and lo! it dies,
    Death's dark eclipse hath dimmèd every ray:
Such eyed the light thy beams untimely shine,
True light sith we have lost, we crave not thine.

THE ASSUMPTION OF OUR LADY.

[Addl. MSS. Brit. Mus. No. 10,422.]

IF sin be captive, grace must find release;
    From curse of sin the innocent is free;
Tomb prison is for sinners that decease,
    No tomb but throne to guiltless doth agree:
Though thralls of sin lie lingering in the grave,
Yet faultless corse with soul reward must have.

The dazzled eye doth dimmèd light require,
    And dying sights repose in shrouding shades;
But eagles' eyes to brightest light aspire,
    And living looks delight in lofty glades:
Faint-wingèd fowl by ground do faintly fly,
Our princely eagle mounts unto the sky.

Gem to her worth, spouse to her love ascends,
    Prince to her throne, queen to her heavenly King,
Whose court with solemn pomp on her attends,
    And quires of saints with greeting notes do sing;
Earth rendereth up her undeservèd prey,
Heaven claims the right, and bears the prize away.

VERSES APPENDED TO "THE TRIUMPHS OVER DEATH."

CLARA ducum soboles, superis nova sedibus hospes,
    Clausit inoffenso tramite puræ diem :
Dotibus ornavit, superavit moribus ortum,
    Omnibus una prior, parfuit una sibi :
Lux genus ingenio, generi lux inclita virtus
    Virtutisque fuit mens generosa decus.
Mors muta at properatæ dies orbemque relinquit,
    Prolem matre verum conjuge flore genus,
Occidit à se alium tulit hic occasus in ortum,
    Vivat, ad occiduas non reditura vices.

Of Howard's stem a glorious branch is dead,
    Sweet lights eclipsèd were at her decease ;
In Buckhurst' line she gracious issue spread,
    She heaven with two, with four did earth increase.
Fame, honour, grace, gave air unto her breath,
Rest, glory, joys, were sequels of her death.

Death aim'd too high, he hit too choice a wight,
    Renowned for birth, for life, for lovely parts ;

He kill'd her cares, he brought her worths to light,
　　He robb'd our eyes, but hath enrich'd our hearts:
Lot let out of her ark a Noah's dove,
But many hearts were arks unto her love.

Grace, Nature, Fortune, did in her conspire
　　To show a proof of their united skill:
Sly Fortune, ever false, did soon retire,
　　But double grace supplied false Fortune's ill.
And though she wrought not unto Fortune's pitch,
In grace and virtue few were found so rich.

Heaven of this heavenly pearl is now possess'd,
　　Whose lustre was the blaze of honour's light,
Whose substance pure of every good the best,
　　Whose price the crown of [every] highest right;
Whose praise, to be herself; whose greatest bliss.
To live, to love, to be where now she is.

VERSES PREFIXED TO "SHORT RULES OF GOOD LIFE," ADDRESSED TO THE CHRISTIAN READER.

I.

IF Virtue be thy guide,
    True comfort is thy path,
And thou secure from erring steps,
    That lead to vengeance wrath.

Not widest open door,
    Nor spacious ways she goes;
To straight and narrow gate and way,
    She calls, she leads, she shows.

She calls, the fewest come;
    She leads the humble sprited,
She shows them rest at race's end,
    Souls' rest to heaven invited.

'Tis she that offers most;
    'Tis she that most refuse;
'Tis she prevents the broad way plagues,
    Which most do wilful choose.

VERSES PREFIXED TO

   Do choose the wide, the broad,
      The left-hand way and gate:
   These Vice applauds, these Virtue loathes,
      And teacheth hers to hate.

   Her ways are pleasant ways,
      Upon the right-hand side;
   And heavenly happy is that soul
      Takes Virtue for her guide.

II.

A Preparative to Prayer.

WHEN thou dost talk with God, (by prayer
    I mean,)
Lift up pure hands, lay down all lust's desires,
Fix thoughts on heaven, present a conscience clear;
   Such holy blame to mercy's throne aspires.
Confess faults' guilt, crave pardon for thy sin;
Tread holy paths, call grace to guide therein.

It is the spirit with reverence must obey
   Our Maker's will, to practise what He taught;
Make not the flesh thy counsel when thou pray,
   'Tis enemy to every virtuous thought;

It is the foe we daily feed and clothe,
It is the prison that the soul doth loathe.

Even as Elias, mounting to the sky,
  Did cast his mantle to the earth behind,
So, when the heart presents the prayer on high,
  Exclude the world from traffic with the mind.
Lips near to God, and ranging heart within,
Is but vain babbling and converts to sin.

Like Abraham, ascending up the hill
  To sacrifice, his servant left below,
That he might act the great Commander's will,
  Without impeach to his obedient blow;
Even so the soul, remote from earthly things,
Should mount salvation's shelter, mercy's wings.

III.

THE EFFECTS OF PRAYER.

THE sun by prayer did cease his course and
    staid;
  The hungry lions fawn'd upon their prey;
A wallèd passage through the sea it made;
  From furious fire it banish'd heat away;
It shut the heavens three years from giving rain,
It open'd heavens, and clouds pour'd down again.

IV.

ENSAMPLES OF OUR SAVIOUR.

OUR Saviour, (pattern of true holiness,)
   Continual pray'd, us by ensample teaching,
When he was baptized in the wilderness,
   In working miracles and in his preaching,
Upon the mount, in garden groves of death,
At his last supper, at his parting breath.

Oh! fortress of the faithful, sure defence,
   In which doth Christians' cognizance consist;
Their victory, their triumph comes from thence,
   So forcible, hell-gates cannot resist:
A thing whereby both angels, clouds and stars,
At man's request fight God's revengeful wars.

Nothing more grateful in the highest eyes,
   Nothing more firm in danger to protect us,
Nothing more forcible to pierce the skies,
   And not depart till mercy do respect us:
And, as the soul life to the body gives,
So prayer revives the soul, by prayer it lives.

APPENDIX.

No. I.

To the worshipful his very good father Mr. R. S. his dutiful son R. S. wisheth all happiness.

IN children of former ages it hath been thought so behoveful a point of duty to their parents, in presence by servicable offices, in absence by other effectual significations, to yield proof of their thankful minds, that neither any child could omit it without touch of ungratefulness, nor the parents forbear it without nice displeasure. But now we are fallen into sore calamity of times, and the violence of heresy hath so crossed this course both of virtue and nature, that these ingrafted laws, never infringed by the most savage and brute creatures, cannot of God's people without peril be observed. I am not of so unnatural a kind, of so wild an education, or so unchristian a spirit, as not to remember the root out of which I branched, or to forget my secondary maker and author of my being. It is not the carelessness of a cold affection, nor the want of a due and reverent respect that has made me such a stranger to my native home, and so backward in defraying the debt of a thankful mind, but only the iniquity of these days, that maketh my presence perilous, and the discharge of my duties an occasion of danger. I was loth to inforce an unwilling courtesy upon any, or, by seeming officious, to become offensive ; deeming it better to let time digest the fear that my return into the realm had bred in my kindred, than abruptly to intrude myself, and to purchase their danger, whose good will I so highly esteem. I never doubted but that the belief, which to all my friends by descent and pedigree is, in a manner, hereditary, framed in them a right persuasion of my present calling, not suffering them to measure their censures of me by the ugly terms and odious epithets wherewith heresy hath sought to discredit my functions, but rather by the reverence of so worthy a sacrament, and the sacred usages of all former ages. Yet, because I might easily perceive by apparent conjectures, that many were more willing to hear of me than from me, and readier to praise than to use my endeavours, I have hitherto bridled my desire to see them by the care and jealousy of their safety ; and banishing myself from the scene of my cradle in my own country, I have lived like a foreigner, finding among strangers that which, in my nearest blood, I presumed not to seek. But now, considering that delay may have qualified fear, and knowing my person only to import danger to others, and my persuasion to none but to myself, I thought it high time to utter my sincere and dutiful mind,

APPENDIX.

and to open a vent to my zealous affection, which I have so long smothered and suppressed in silence. For not only the original law of nature written in all children's hearts, and derived from the breast of their mother, is a continual solicitude urging me in your behalf, but the sovereign decree enacted by the Father of heaven, ratified by His Son, and daily repeated by the instinct of the Holy Ghost, bindeth every child in the due of Christianity to tender the state and welfare of his parents, and is a motive that alloweth no excuse, but of necessity presseth to performance of duty. Nature by grace is not abolished, nor destroyed, but perfected; neither are the impressions razed or annulled, but suited to the ends of grace and nature. And if its affections be so forcible, that even in hell, where rancour and despite, and all feelings of goodness are overwhelmed by malice, they moved the rich glutton by experience of his own misery, to have compassion of his kindred, how much more in the Church of God, where grace quickeneth, charity inflameth, and nature's good inclinations are abetted by supernatural gifts, ought the like piety to prevail. And, who but those more merciless than damned creatures, would see their dearest friends plunged in the like perils, and not be wounded by deep remorse at their lamentable and imminent hazard? If in beholding a mortal enemy wrought and tortured with deadly pains, the strongest heart softeneth with some sorrows; if the most frozen and fierce mind cannot but thaw and melt with pity even when it knows such person to suffer his deserved torments; how much less can the heart of a child consider those that bred him into this world, to be in the fall to far more bitter extremities, and not bleed with grief at their uncomfortable case. Surely, for mine own part, though I challenge not the prerogative of the best disposition, yet am I not of so harsh and churlish a humour, but that it is a continual corrective and cross unto me, that, whereas my endeavours have reclaimed many from the brink of perdition, I have been less able to employ them, where they were most due; and was barred from affording to my dearest friends that which hath been eagerly sought and beneficially obtained by mere strangers. Who hath more interest in the grape than he who planted the vine? who more right to the crop than he who sowed the corn? or where can the child owe so great service as to him to whom he is indebted for his very life and being? With young Tobias I have travelled far, and brought home a freight of spiritual substance to enrich you, and medicinable receipts against your ghostly maladies. I have, with Esau, after long toil in pursuing a long and painful chace, returned with the full prey, you were wont to love; desiring thereby to insure your blessing. I have in this general famine of all true and Christian food, with Joseph, prepared abundance of the bread of angels for the repast of your soul. And now my desire is that my drugs may cure you, my prey delight you, and my provision

APPENDIX.

feed you, by whom I have been cured, enlightened, and fed myself; that your courtesies may, in part, be countervailed, and my duty, in some sort, performed. Despise not, good Sire, the youth of your son, neither deem your God measureth his endowments by number of years. Hoary senses are often couched under youthful locks, and some are riper in the spring, than others in the autumn of their age. God chose not Esau himself, nor his eldest son, but young David to conquer Goliah and to rule his people: not the most aged person, but Daniel, the most innocent youth, delivered Susannah from the iniquity of the judges. Christ, at twelve years of age, was found in the temple questioning with the greatest doctors. A true Elias can conceive, that a little cloud may cast a large and abundant shower; and the scripture teacheth us, that God unveileth to little ones that which He concealeth from the wisest sages. His truth is not abashed by the minority of the speaker; for out of the mouths of infants and sucklings He can perfect His praises. Timothy was young, and yet a principal pastor: St. John, a youth, and yet an apostle; yea, and the angels by appearing in youthful semblance, gave us a proof that many glorious gifts may be shrouded under tender shapes. All this, I say, not to claim any privileges surmounting the rate of usual abilities, but to avoid all touch of presumption in advising my elders; seeing that it hath the warrant of scripture, the testimony of example, and sufficient grounds both in grace and nature. There is a diversity in the degrees of carnal consanguinity; and the pre-eminence appertaineth unto you, as superior over your child: yet if you consider our alliance in the chief portion, I mean the soul, which differenceth man from inferior creatures, we are of equal proximity to our heavenly Father, both descended from the same parent, and with no other distance in our degrees, but that you are the eldest brother. Seeing, therefore, that your superiority is founded on flesh and blood, think it, I pray you, no dishonour to your age, nor disparagement to your person, if, with all humility, I offer my advice unto you. One man cannot be perfect in all qualities, neither is it a disgrace to the goldsmith if he be ignorant of the carpenter's trade; many are deep lawyers, and yet small divines: many very clever in feats of body, and curious in external accomplishments, yet little experienced in matters of mind. For these many years I have studied and practised spiritual medicine, acquainting myself with the beating and temper of every pulse, and travailing in the cure of maladies incident to souls. If, therefore, I proffer you the fruit of my long studies, and make you a present of my profession, I hope you will construe it rather as a dutiful part, than as any point of presumption. He may be a father to the soul that is a son to the body, and requite the benefit of his temporal life by reviving his parent from a spiritual death. And to this effect did Christ say, *My mother and brethren are they that do the will of*

APPENDIX.

my Father which is in heaven: upon which words St. Climacus shows on what kindred a Christian ought chiefly to rely. "Let him," he says, "be thy Father, that both can and will disburthen thee of the weight of thy sins." Such a Father as this Saint speaketh of, may you have in your own son, to enter your family in the pre-recited affinity; of which happily it was a significant presage, a boding of the future event, that, even from my infancy, you were wont, in merriment, to call me your father: now this is the customary style allotted to my present estate.* Now, therefore, to join issue and to come to the principal drift of my discourse; most humbly and earnestly I am to beseech you, that, both in respect of the honour of God, your duty to His Church, the comfort of your children, and the redress of your own soul, you would seriously consider the terms you stand in, and weigh yourself in a Christian balance, taking for your counterpoise the judgments of God. Take heed in time, that the word Thekel, written of old against Balthazar and interpreted by young Daniel, be not verified in you; remember the exposition, "you have been weighed in the balance and found wanting." Remember that you are in the balance, that the date of your pilgrimage is well nigh expired, and that it now behoveth you to look forward to your country. Your strength languisheth, your senses become impaired, and your body

---

* Being a Father of the Society of Jesus.

droopeth, and on every side the ruinous cottage of your faint and feeble flesh threateneth a fall. Having so many harbingers of death, to pre-admonish you of your end, how can you but prepare for so dreadful a stranger. The young may die quickly, but the old cannot live long. The young man's life by casualty may be abridged, but the old man's life can by no physic be long augmented. And, therefore, if green years must sometimes think of the grave, the thoughts of sere age should continually dwell on the same. The prerogative of infancy is innocency; of childhood, reverence; of manhood maturity, and of age wisdom; and seeing that the chief property of wisdom is to be mindful of things past, careful of things present, and provident of things to come, use now the privilege of nature's talent to the benefit of your soul, and strive hereafter to be wise in well-doing, and watchful in foresight of future harms. To serve the world you are now unable, and, though you were able, you have little wish to do so, seeing that it never gave you but an unhappy welcome, a hurtful entertainment, and now doth abandon you with an unfortunate farewell. You have long sowed in a field of flint which could bring you nothing forth but a crop of cares and afflictions of spirit, rewarding your labours with remorse, and for your pains repaying you with eternal damages. It is now more than a seasonable time to alter your course of so unthriving a husbandry, and to enter into the fields of God's Church; in which, sowing the seed of repentant sorrow, and watering it with the tears of humble contrition, you may reap a more beneficial harvest, and gather the fruit of everlasting consolation. Remember, I pray you, that your spring is spent, and your summer overpast; you are now arrived at the fall of the leaf, yea the winter-colours have already stained your hoary head.

Be not careless, saith St. Augustine, though our loving Lord bear long with offenders; for the longer He stayeth without finding amendment, the sorer will He punish when He cometh to judgment; His patience, in so long expecting, is only to lend us respite to repent, not any way to enlarge our leisure to sin. He that is tossed with variety of storms, and cannot reach his destined port, maketh not much way, but is sore turmoiled; so he that passeth many years and purchaseth little profit, hath had a long being, but a short life: for life is more to be measured by merit than by number of days, seeing that most men by many days do but procure many deaths, while others in short space attain a life of infinite ages. What is the body without the soul, but a mass of corruption; and what the soul without God but a sepulchre of sin? If God be the way, the truth and the life, he that goeth without Him, strayeth, he that liveth without Him dieth, and he that is not taught by Him erreth. Well saith St. Augustine, that God is our true and chief life, from whom to revolt is to fall,

APPENDIX.

and to return is to rise. Be not you, therefore, of the number of those who begin not to live until they be ready to die, and then after a foe's desert, come to crave of God a friend's entertainment. Some think to share heaven in a moment, which the best scarce attain in the godliness of many years: and when they have glutted themselves with worldly delights, they would fain pass at once from the diet of Dives to the crown of Lazarus, and from the servitude of Satan to the freedom of the Saints. But be you well assured, God is not so penurious of friends as to hold Himself and His kingdom for the refuse and reversion of their lives, who have sacrificed the principal thereof to His enemies and their own brutal appetites; then only ceasing to offend, when the ability of offending is taken from them. True it is that a thief may be saved upon the cross and find mercy at the last gasp, but well, saith St. Augustine, that though it be possible, yet is it scarce credible, that his death should find favour whose whole life hath deserved wrath; and that his repentance should be accepted, which more through fear of hell and love of himself than love of God, or hatred of sin, crieth for mercy. Wherefore, good Sire, make no longer delay, but being so near the breaking up of your mortal house, take time, before straitened by extremity, to satisfy God's justice. Though you suffered the bud to be blasted, and the flower to fade; though you permitted the fruit to perish and the leaves to wither away; yea, though you let the boughs decay, and the very trunk corrupt, yet, alas! keep life in the root for fear the whole become fuel for the fire. Death hath already spoiled you of the better part of your natural force, and hath left you now to the last lease of your expiring days; the remainder whereof, as it cannot be long, so doth it warn you speedily to ransom your former losses. What is age but a kalendar of death, and what doth your present weakness import, but an earnest of your approaching dissolution? You are now embarked on your final voyage, and not far off from the stinted period of your course, therefore, be not dispurveyed of such proper provisions as are behoveful in so perplexed and perilous a journey. Death in itself is very fearful, but much more terrible in regard of the judgment that it summoneth us unto. If you were stretched on your departing bed, burthened with the heavy load of your former trespasses and gored with the sting of a festered conscience; if you felt the hand of Death grasping your heart's-strings and ready to make the rueful divorce between body and soul; if you lay panting for breath and bathed in a cold and fatal sweat, wearied with struggling against the pangs of death, oh, how much would you give for one hour of repentance, at what a rate would you value one day's contrition! Worlds would then be worthless in respect of a little respite; a short time would seem more precious than the treasures of empires. Nothing would be so much esteemed as a moment of time, which is now by months and years so lavishly

APPENDIX.

misspent. Oh! how deeply would it wound your heart, when looking back into yourself, you consider many faults committed and not confessed, many good works omitted or not recovered, your service to God promised but never performed. How intolerable will be your case! your friends are fled, your servants frightened, your thoughts amazed, your memory distracted, your whole mind aghast and unable to perform what it would, only your guilty conscience will continually upbraid you with most bitter accusations. What will be your thoughts, when, stripped of your mortal body, and turned both out of the service and house-room of this world, you are forced to enter into uncouth and strange paths, and with unknown and ugly company to be carried before a most severe judge, carrying in your own conscience your judgment written, and a perfect register of all your misdeeds; when you shall see *Him* prepared to pass the sentence upon you, against whom you have transgressed; he is to be the umpire, whom by so many offences you have made your enemy; when not only the devils, but even the angels will plead against you, and yourself, in spite of your will, be your own sharpest impeacher. What would you do in these dreadful exigencies, when you saw the ghastly dungeon and huge gulf of hell breaking out with most fearful flames? when you heard the weeping and gnashing of teeth, the rage of those hellish monsters, the horror of the place, the rigour of the pain, the terror of the company, and the eternity of the punishments? Would you then think them wise that would delay in such weighty matters, and idly play away a time allotted to prevent such intolerable calamities? Would you then account it secure to nurse in your bosom a brood of serpents, or suffer your soul to entertain so many accusers? Would not you, then, think a whole life too little to do penance for so many iniquities? Why then do you not, at least, devote the small remnant and surplus of these your latter days in seeking to make an atonement with God, and in freeing your conscience from the corruption that, by your treason and fall, has crept into it; whose very eyes that read this discourse, and very understanding that conceiveth it, shall be cited as certain witnesses of what I describe. Your soul will then experience the most terrible fears, if you do not recover yourself into the fold and family of God's Church. What have you gained by being so long enslaved to the world? What interest have you reaped that can equal your detriment in grace and virtue? You cannot be now inveigled with the passions of youth to make a partial estimate of things, and set no difference between counterfeit and current, for they are now either worn out by the touch of time, or falling into reproof by the trial of their own folly. It cannot be fear that leadeth you amiss, seeing it were so unfitting a thing that any craven cowardice of flesh and blood should daunt the prowess of an intelligent man, who, by his wisdom, cannot but discern how much more cause there is to fear God than man, and to stand in more awe of perpetual than of temporal penalties. An ungrounded presumption on the mercy of God, and the hope of His assistance at the last plunge—the ordinary device of the devil—is too palpable a collusion to mislead a sound and sensible man. Who would trust eternal affairs upon the gliding slipperiness and shifting current of an uncertain life? or who, but one of distempered mind, would attempt to cheat the decipherer of all thoughts, with whom we may dissemble, but whom to deceive is impossible? Shall we esteem it cunning to rob the time from Him and bestow it on His enemies, who keepeth account of the last moment of life, and will examine in the end how that moment hath been employed? It is a preposterous policy to attempt to fight against God. It were a strange piece of art, and a device of exorbitant folly, while the ship is sound, the pilot well, the sailors strong, the gale favourable, to lie idle in the roads; yet when the ship leaked, the pilot lay sick, the mariners faint, the storm boisterous, and the sea in a tumult of outrageous surges, then to launch forth, to hoist up sail, and to set out for a voyage into far countries; yet such is the skill of those cunning repenters, whose thoughts in soundness of health, and in the perfect use of reason, cannot resolve to cut the cables and weigh the anchors that withhold them from God. Nevertheless they feed themselves with a fond presumption that, when their senses are astounded, their minds distracted, their understanding confused, and both their body and mind racked and tormented with the throbs of a mortal sickness, that then, forsooth, they will think of the weightiest matters, and become sudden saints, when they are scarce able to behave themselves like reasonable creatures. If neither the canon, civil, nor common law alloweth a man, punished in judgment, to make any testament or bequest of his temporal substance, being then presumed to be less than a man; how can he that is distracted with an unsettled conscience, distrained with the fits of his dying flesh, and maimed in all his faculties, be thought of such due discretion as to dispose of his chiefest inheritance, the treasure of his soul, and the concerns of a whole eternity in so short and stormy a moment? No, no: they that will loiter in the seed time, and only begin to sow when others reap; they that will riot out their health, and cast their accounts when they can scarcely speak; they that will slumber out the day, and enter on their journey when the light faileth them, let them blame their own folly if they die in debt, and fall headlong into the lapse of endless perdition.

O, dear Sire, remember that the scripture terms it a fearful thing to fall into the hands of the living God, who is able to crush the proud spirit of the obstinate, and to make His enemies the footstool of His feet. Wrestle no longer against the struggles of your own conscience, and the forcible admonitions that God doth send you.

Embrace His mercy before the time of rigour, and return to His Church, lest He debar you His kingdom. He cannot have God for his father that refuseth to possess the Catholic Church for his mother; neither can he attain to the Church triumphant in heaven, who is not a member of the Church militant upon earth. You have been, alas! too long an alien in the tabernacles of sinners, and strayed too far from the folds of God's Church. Turn now the bias of your heart towards the sanctuary of salvation and the city of refuge, seeking the recovery of your wandering steps from the paths of error. Return with a swift force, and hasten with jealous progress to Christian perfection; redeeming the time because the days are evil. The full of your spring-tide is now fallen, and the stream of your life waneth to a low ebb; your tired bark beginneth to leak, and grateth oft upon the gravel of the grave; therefore it is high time for you to strike sail and put into harbour, lest, remaining in the scope of the winds and waves of this wicked time, some unexpected gust should dash you upon the rock of eternal ruin. Tender the pitiful state of your poor soul, and henceforth be more fearful of hell than of persecution, and more eager of heaven than of worldly repose. Had the pen that wrote this letter been dipped in the wounds of the Saviour, and His precious blood been used instead of ink; had one of the highest seraphims come in the most solemn embassy to deliver it unto you, do you not think that it would have strained your heart, and wrought upon your mind to fulfil the contents, and alter your course according to the tenor thereof? Doubtless you will not deny it. Then, good Sire, let it now take the same effect, seeing the difference has been in the ceremonies and not in the substance; and that very God, who should then have invited you to your correction, saith of such as I am, though most unworthy, *He that heareth you, heareth Me; and he that despiseth you, despiseth Me!* I exhort you, therefore, as the vicegerent of God, and I humbly request you as a dutiful child that you would surrender your assent, and yield your soul a happy captive to God's merciful inspirations, proceeding from an infinite love, and tending to your assured good. I have expressed not only my own, but the earnest desire of your other children, whose humble wishes are here written with my pen. For it is a general grief that filleth all our hearts, whom it hath pleased God to shroud under His merciful wing, to see our dearest Father, to whom both nature hath bound and your merits fastened our affection, dismembered from the body to which we are united, to be in hazard of a farther and more grievous separation. O, good Sire, shall so many of your branches enjoy the quickening sap of God's Church, and, shooting up higher towards heaven, bring forth the flowers and fruits of salvation; and, you that are the root of us, lie barren and fruitless? Shall the beams be bright, and the sun eclipsed? Shall the brooks be clear, and the head-spring troubled? Your lot hath no such affinity with the nature of a phœnix that you should reap your offspring from your own ruins; you are not so tied in the straits of the pelican as to revive your issue by murdering yourself; neither we a generation of vipers that cannot come to life but by our parent's destruction. Yea, rather it is the thing we have chiefly in request, that we may be as near linked in spiritual, as we are in natural consanguinity; and, that living with you in the compass of our Church, we may, to our unspeakable comfort, enjoy in heaven your most desired company. Blame me not, good Father, if zeal of your recovery has carried me beyond the limits of a letter. So important a truth cannot be too much avowed, nor too many means used to draw a soul out of the misery of schism. Howsoever, therefore, the soft gales of your morning pleasures lulled you in slumbers; howsoever the violent heat of noon might awake affections, yet now in the cool and calm of the evening retire to a Christian rest, and close up the day of your life with a clear sunset; that leaving all darkness behind you, and carrying in your conscience the light of grace, you may escape the horror of eternal night, and pass from the day of mortality to the Sabbath of everlasting rest: and humbly desiring that my sincere affection may find excuse of my boldness, I here conclude.

APPENDIX.

II.

Letter written to his Brother.

UNDERSTANDING that you were resolved upon a course which most nearly toucheth the salvation of your soul, I received such contentment as a sincere and most faithful love feeleth in the long desired happiness of so dear a friend. But hearing since, that you will dwell in danger and linger in new delays, my hopes hang in suspense, and my heart in grief, angry with the chains that thus enthral you, and sorry to see you captive to your own fears. Shrine not any longer a dead soul in a living body: bail reason out of senses' prison, that after so long a bondage in sin, you may enjoy your former liberty in God's Church, and free your thought from the servile awe of uncertain perils. If all should take effect, that your timorous surmises suggest, yet could not even the misery of your present estate, with the loss of your patronage, and keeping you in this disfavour of God, have either left you any greater benefit to lose, or any deeper infelicity to incur. Weigh with yourself at how easy a price you rate God, whom you are content to sell for the use of your substance, yea, and for the preventing a loss which haply will never ensue. Have you so little need of Him, that you can so long forbear Him? or is He so worthless in your estimation that you will venture nothing for Him? Adjourn not, I pray you, a matter of such importance. Remember that one sin begetteth another, and when you yield to nurse daily this venomous brood in your breast, what can you look for, but, that like vipers, they should compass your destruction. Custom soon groweth to a second nature, and being once master of the mind, it can hardly be cast out of possession. If to-day you find yourself faint, fainter you are like to be to-morrow, if you languish in the same distaste without cure, and suffer the corrosive of sin to consume you without opposing its violence. How can you flatter yourself with an ungrounded hope of mercy, since to continue in it so long, is the surest way to stop the fountain of it for ever? The more you offend God, the less you deserve His favour; and to be deaf when He calleth you, is to close His ears against all cries in the time of your necessity. If you mean to surrender your heart to Him, why do you lend so much leisure to the devil to strengthen his hold; and why stop up the passages with mire by which the pure waters of grace must flow into your soul? Look if you can upon a crucifix without blushing; do but count the five wounds of Christ once over without a bleeding conscience. Read your sins in those characters, and examine your thoughts whether the sight do please them. Alas! if that innocent blood move you not, or if you can find still in your heart to open afresh such undeserved wounds, I would I might send you the

APPENDIX.

sacrifice of my dearest veins, to try whether nature could awake remorse, and prepare a way for grace's entrance. Sorrow puts me to silence, and therefore, Brother, I must end, desiring you to have pity on yourself, whose harms make so bitter an impression on Ager's mind. God of His infinite goodness strengthen you in all your good designments.

III.

STATE PAPER OFFICE, DONCASTER. No. 190.

Endorsed: Mr. Topcliffe about Mr. Bellamy, Septem. 1592.

IT may please yo' Lo. At my retorne out of the cuntrie this night, I did heare y' Mr. Bellamyes too dowghters are comitted to the gayt howse. But the old hene that hatched these chickens (the worst that ever was) is yett at a lodginge: Lett her be sent to the prison there at the gayt howse, and severd from her dowghters, and her spons Thomas Bellamye comitted to S. Katheryns, And yow shall heare prooved cause enough, and see it woorke a straundge example (hereaboutts).

But ne' Younge nor other cŏmyssyoner must knowe that I do knowe the rest, or am a doer in this devyce. Nor by my will other than his Lordship that was w' yow when yow did concluyde what should be done at grenwidge last.

Lett them feele a day or too impresonment, And then your Lo: shall see me play the partt of a trew man, w. charity in the end, to the honor of the stayt; and so in hast at mydnight this fryday,

Y' Lo: at comandement,
RIC: TOPCLYFFE.

To the right honor, my Lorde
Sir John Puckering, Lorde
Keeper of the Great Seale
of Englande.

IV.

STATE PAPER OFFICE, DONCASTER. No. 197.

Endorsed: The exaiation of Mrs. Bellamye and her three children.

THE EXAMINATION of Katheryne Bellamye wiffe of Richard Bellamye of 'harrowchill taken before me Richard Yonge the xviijth day of Julye 1594.

The said ex' saieth that she dothe goe to churche, and dothe heare dyvine service and sermons, but she saieth that she hath not receyved the communyon.

Itm, she saieth that she hathe twoe sonnes, one ffaithe, and thother Thomas, and they doe goe to churche everye Sondaye.

APPENDIX. xxiii

Itm, she saieth that she hath twoe dawghters, one called Awdrye, thother Marye, and they be in howse w' her, but they doe not goe to churche.

Itm, she saieth that Mr. Willm. Page* her uncle dothe lodge at her howse and dothe not goe to churche.

Thomas Bellamye off thage of 22 or 23 years exaied saith that he goeth to churche, and heareth dyvyne service, and sermons alsoe. And althoughe he did not receyve the comunyon the last Easter, yet nowe he is willinge; he saith also that Mr. Willm. Page lyeth at his ffather's, but goeth not to churche.

Awdrye Wylford wydowe exaied saieth, that she remayneth w' her mother Mrs. Bellayme, and beinge asked whether she goeth to Churche, answereth noe, and saith that her conscience will not give her to goe to churche, and (so farr as she can remember) she was nev' at churche in alle her lyfe tyme, and refuseth also now to goe, or to have conference.

Marye Bellamye of thage of 27 years exaied saith, that she hath dwelt alwaies w' her Mother, and hathe not been at churche these 14 yeares; And being asked why? saith that

---

* Two members of the Page family, Antony and Francis, both priests and the latter S.J. were executed; the former in 1593, the latter in 1692.—*Vide Chaloner's Memoirs of Missionary Priests.*

APPENDIX.

her conscience will not suffer her, neither will she nowe goe to churche, or yet admytte anye conference.

Endorsed : the exaiacon of Mrs. Bellamye and her three children.

FINIS.

www.ingramcontent.com/pod-product-compliance
Lightning Source LLC
Chambersburg PA
CBHW031815220426
43662CB00007B/664